# Home and Abroad
## Women Write of Spirit, Memory, and Place

Compiled by
Maureen Breitzmann
Virginia Broich
Jean Comstock
Marla Kapperud
Laura Langer

WILLERNIE
‹PRESS›

FIRST WILLERNIE PRESS EDITION, DECEMBER 2005
Copyright © 2005 Willernie Press

All rights reserved under International and Pan-American Copyright Conventions. Published in the United States by Willernie Press, Minneapolis, MN. All rights to individual essays retained by the authors.

Willernie is a registered trademark and Willernie Press and colophon are trademarks of Willernie Press, Inc. (SAN 256-8993)

Library of Congress Control Number: 2005931725

Willernie ISBN: 978-0-9771563-0-3

*Design by Laura Langer*

*Cover Photo © Marla Kapperud 2005*
*"Barbecue at Elm Creek Park Reserve"*

Printed in the United States of America

1 3 5 7 9 8 6 4 2

# TABLE OF CONTENTS

Foreword

| | |
|---|---|
| Visiting A Roman Family<br>by Mary McConnon | 1 |
| Bridesmaids in Belize<br>by Kelly Westhoff | 3 |
| The Art of Skipping Rocks<br>by Maureen Breitzmann | 7 |
| Wyoming Revival<br>by Maggie Delfosse | 11 |
| Murveil Curfew<br>by Gina Briefs-Elgin | 13 |
| The Stamp Sands<br>by Laura Langer | 17 |
| The Glasgow Monk<br>by Jean Comstock | 21 |

Kiss and Tell: The Tale of a Magical Parade       25
    by Maureen Breitzmann

Roots and Wings                                    29
    by Mary Louise Poquette

It Only Takes a Moment                             33
    by Jean Comstock

The BWCA                                           37
    by Diane Klein Smith

The Best Sights in London:                         41
Traveling with Daughters
    by Karen Ackerman

Voodoo                                             45
    by Jane Congdon

Lauri                                              49
    by Brenda Wolfe

Dachau                                             51
    by Virginia A Broich

Birthdays and Umbrellas                            55
    by Susan Slater Blythe

Lost in Pepper Town                                57
    by Laura Langer

Strolling with Mr. Zhue                            61
    by Virginia A. Broich

| | |
|---|---|
| Zywiec<br>    by Marla Kapperud | 65 |
| My Father's Bar-B-Que<br>    by Karen Ackerman | 69 |
| Beers of My Life: Amstel to Zywiec<br>    by Marla Kapperud | 73 |
| Putti<br>    by Gina Briefs-Elgin | 79 |
| Reclamation<br>    by Pamela Mittlefehldt | 83 |
| Death Toll Mounts in Vietnam<br>    by Catherine Watson | 87 |

Acknowledgements

Contributors

# Foreword

On Sunday, July 18, 2004, sixteen women from around the United States converged on the Minneapolis campus of the University of Minnesota. They were about to embark on a week's journey, exploring their shared passions of writing and travel in a Split Rock Arts Program entitled, "Writing the Travel Memoir: Spirit, Place, and Change."

For many of us, the instructor, Catherine Watson, was our primary motivation. Those coming from outside Minnesota, without the weekly privilege of reading Watson's work in the Star Tribune, were about to meet a most generous, authentic journalist and person. An award-winning journalist and long-time travel editor of the Star Tribune in Minneapolis, Catherine showed us the best traits of mentoring and teaching. She helped us see the stories we hold within, introduced us to ourselves as travel writers, and left us with the advice to always "write fiercely."

This book is a result of the class. Every participant submitted at least one essay, sharing humor, memories, dreams, fears, and every other emotion that makes each of us a traveler, whether we stir from our comfortable chairs in the living room or not.

As you share our journeys, we hope you discover something about yourself and the amazing stories you have yet to tell.

# Visiting a Roman Family
## by Mary McConnon

Choosing to live with a family when you travel abroad is a chance to see normal family life in another country. But sometimes the family turns out to be not so normal. It is also why I have been to Rome three times and never seen the Sistine Chapel. Life in the Roman family I visit becomes all encompassing.

IN 1963, WHEN I LEFT THE MIDWEST for my first trip overseas, I stayed with Anna, my family's AFS exchange student, who lives in Rome. Her family was wealthy and prominent I found out. They were also a moveable feast of characters—Anna, her husband, Luciano, her parents, her sister and brother-in-law, her brother, the maid, a big brown family dog, and now me.

Everyone in the family did everything together in a group, with a changeable cast, but always in a ceremonial fashion, never spontaneously. For example, when it was announced that we would all go shopping in the center city, everyone stood in the foyer and debated which liqueur to drink before leaving on the shopping trip. There were at least twenty small, brightly-colored bottles in a row on a shelf in the living room to choose from. The liqueur was finally consumed after a forty-five minute wait, and we all left. Shopping in Rome, I guess, must be stressful.

Then there was the way the family watched TV. Everyone in the family grabbed a dining room chair and moved into the living room. The chairs were lined up in front of the TV by rank. In the front row were the mother and father. The middle row was Anna, Luciano, and me. Behind us were Anna's brother, sister, and brother-in-law. In the last row was Giulia, the maid. The dog stayed back in the dining room, asleep under the table.

When "I Love Lucy" came on, the entire family was silent and respectful, not producing a single laugh, since they took the program totally seriously because it was about a family. In contrast, Dr. Kildare was perceived as a comedy. Who, they thought, could possibly take a doctor seriously? This included the sister and brother-in-law who are both doctors.

The first dinner I ate with Anna's family started out with the whole cast of characters conversing in a tone just short of yelling. The tone only grew louder as the meal progressed. After we were seated, Anna informed me that she would not translate what people were saying. I was a little bit scared by the thought of sitting through a whole meal while people were yelling and not understanding a word they were saying.

Anna then explained that she worked as a simultaneous translator and was tired of translating. Besides, she predicted, there was always the same conversation every day at the dinner table. When would her brother join the family furniture business? Who was feeding the family dog under the table? Eventually, someone would get out the joke magazine and tell a new joke. All this was happening in a large family apartment in a ritzy neighborhood in Rome, Italy, in a wealthy and prominent family.

Just as Anna predicted, the father and son quarreled, and the volume of the conversation grew louder. The joke magazine came out, and the conversation grew even louder. This is the kind of joke they were telling at the dinner table. Anna did translate this. I was shocked.

A man in a small town goes to the doctor for a physical. The doctor asks him the usual questions about his family life. "Fine," was the reply. His job was also "fine." His sex life was "Fine, about once a week." The doctor exclaimed, "That's not enough for an Italian man." The man taking the physical replied, "Why, I thought I was doing really well for a priest in a small town."

Someone really was feeding the dog under the table.

I never did find out who.

# Bridesmaids in Belize
## by Kelly Westhoff

*E*ven in Belize, bridesmaid dresses are ugly. The unfortunate Belizean bridesmaids I happened across donned full-skirted ordeals of sunshine yellow with matching ribbons in their hair. As further insult, the young women carried durable, plastic flowers—sunflowers, to match, of course.

The bridesmaids outshone the bride. I saw the bride—I just don't remember what she looked like. I saw the groom as well. He was equally drab. Instead, eyes, and then actual bodies, were drawn to the bridesmaids like moths to the sun. Wedding guests, townspeople, and tourists alike followed the yellow skirts.

It was just a block and a half from the Catholic church to the reception at the San Pedro Lion's Club. San Pedro is the one and only town on the Belizean island of Ambergris Caye. The town is a dusty little place with a population that would easily fit inside an American mall. My husband and I were there for a week of relaxation and had chosen Ambergris Caye based on its guidebook description: quaint, quiet, and welcoming to strangers.

San Pedro had three streets: Front Street, Middle Street, and Back Street. Front Street was closest to the beach, Middle Street came next, and Back Street was last. A series of smaller roads cut perpendicular to the streets, connecting the town in a grid. We walked the town every night after dinner, making it up and down each street two or three times before an hour passed. It was a Saturday night and in our strolling we had run into the wedding.

The wedding guests were just spilling from the church into Front Street the first time we walked by. The next time we passed, the bridesmaids were there along with a flower girl, also in yellow, and the priest. By the third time, it was clear that the party was moving down a block to the Lion's Club. The bridesmaids led the way, but the music had already started pulling people in.

The Lion's Club was for wedding guests only, but three of its four walls were half walls—concrete on the bottom, open to the street on top. The remaining wall was a full wall. This was where the stage had been set up. The band was a reggae group. Three black men in their twenties sang on stage. They sported matching Hawaiian shirts and do-rags on their heads.

Across the street from the Lion's Club was an ice cream shop. My husband and I had discovered Manelly's our first night in San Pedro and revisited the shop each night. Ice cream was always a good choice as far as we were concerned. What a bonus that this night live music was playing in the street. We joined the line for ice cream, which backed up inside to the door, and planned our flavors.

Double chocolate and mango sorbet in hand, we headed back to the street, found a free spot on the curb, and sat down to watch the wedding reception across the street. As the guests sat down to eat, however, the wedding grew boring. The real action was on the street just outside the Lion's Club. Here, the uninvited gathered. The music was free, the ice cream nearby, and the night was just beginning.

Young couples passed with toddlers tripping along behind. Kids on bicycles zoomed around the block, a flash then gone, a flash then gone again. Ten-year-old boys, ice cream on their cheeks and scabs on their knees, ran in and out of Manelly's with coins in hand; in the back of the store was a row of video games.

Most of the people were barefoot. Before we'd arrived, I'd read in a guide that San Pedro had just decided to pave its streets in 1999. The guide was wrong. None of the streets were paved. Instead they were ribbons of dusty beach sand blown in from the sea. Blacktop may have been hidden underneath, but it didn't seem to matter. Sand was softer on the feet and in a town where the people seemed to prefer life without shoes, this was just as well.

Some of the townspeople were wearing shoes that night. A band of middle school girls promenaded before us, each one in strappy, platform sandals. They strutted in cliques of three or four dressed in off-the-shoulder halters and skirts so tight we could guess the color of their underwear. They were pouty with tiny paunches of bellies. Their skin was every shade between hot chocolate and coffee cream.

One girl in particular caught our eye. She strolled the block between

# Bridesmaids in Belize

Manelly's and the Lion's Club, switching cliques to move up the street again when the previous group stayed put. She was scantly dressed, yet modest: a gleaming Virgin Mary medallion hung from her slim neck and rested on her chest just above the curve of her pink spaghetti strap tank.

The band moved fluidly from one tune to the next. My husband and I tried to catch the lyrics, but they were lost to us. The singers jammed in a language other than English, other than Spanish—the Creole, probably, that we heard islanders speak when tourists weren't around.

When a new song started, the girl in the pink spaghetti strap tank danced in the middle of the street. Her hips tipped, her nape swayed, she all out boogied. Then she stopped, flipped her chin-length brown bob, and cast an anxious glance to a group of young men on the corner.

This is what I love most about travel. I love these slivers of time when foreignness falls away, when language doesn't count, when religion is insignificant, and government is mute. These moments reveal mundane universal truths: bridesmaid dresses are ugly, and thirteen-year-olds desperately want to be cool no matter where we live. Slivers of life in another land, when people are being good and joyous and kind, prove my humanness to me. Despite all that separates me from them, their humanness is right there before me. This is when I believe in a divine.

At home it is easy to forget what I share with a middle school girl in San Pedro town. Instead I watch the news and shake my head. Will the bickering and fighting ever stop? Can't everyone see that we are all just the same? Yet this is so easy to say and so easy to forget, so hard to believe. But wedding parties in Belize make me believe it.

The young men hanging out on the corner looked good. They were a few years older than the middle school girls fawning at them. In total, there were seven. Two perched atop the fence of a restaurant; another straddled the curb, one foot on the sidewalk, one foot in the street. One young man reclined on a bike, his legs stiff ahead of him and dug into the sand. The rest loitered on the hood of a golf cart parked nearby.

Their jeans were baggy, their shoes flashed Nike, and their shirts were brashly-colored jerseys—the Bulls, the Heat, the Jazz. A couple of them flipped their sunglasses up on top of their heads; one twirled his slowly around in circles by an earpiece. They looked like they were up to no good except they weren't doing anything wrong. They were simply out to see and be seen, but they certainly weren't trading glances with the girl in the pink spaghetti strap tank. And they'd never stoop so low as to lock eyes with two gringos licking ice cream on the curb.

# The Art of Skipping Rocks
## by Maureen Breitzmann

*T*here is an art to skipping rocks that you may be unaware of if you do not hail from a place where the water only appears to end because your eyes can only see so far.

I was lucky enough to grow up in Superior, Wisconsin, a struggling, stagnating city perched on the nation's best real estate: Lake Superior. The lake is where we swam as kids, how we gauged the weather, and why I am drawn to that city as a child to anything sweet.

I don't particularly like swimming in the water anymore. I much prefer the security of swimming in an indoor pool, for I fear the mystery the surface conceals. I do, however, cherish the very sight of it.

Lake Superior is a canvas for sparkling gems of light on sunny days, with calm ripples barely disturbing its serene reflection. On stormy days, winds invoke angry whitecaps that punctuate the dark waters and attack the shore in violent protest.

It is mighty. It is lovely. It is home.

I recently made the drive up Interstate 35 from my apartment in St. Paul to see my dad and niece, Schyler, who was visiting for the week. With only a weekend to spend, I threw out many ideas that were quickly rejected and, in the end, the lake won. We decided to take a drive up Minnesota's North Shore to explain to Schyler our love affair with a body of water.

My dad grew up in Superior, so his entire life was spent as the lake's neighbor. And while he openly curses how the lake wind stunts his raspberries and kills his corn, I know he would live in no other place.

It had been a long time since he visited the lake, but the very thought of it seemed to breathe life into him that I never knew was missing. He got ready quickly and volunteered to drive despite his hatred for traffic and unwillingness to drive in the comparatively big city of Duluth.

Our day began in Duluth's Canal Park. We were going to skip rocks. It was clear, but chilly and, though it was June, I longed for a pair of mittens. The first steps onto the beach brought unmistakable sounds—the grinding of stones against each other as they allowed for our weight, the squawking of seagulls, the waves' rhythmic caressing of shore.

I hadn't been rock skipping since I was much younger. After my parents divorced, my dad used to take me on long walks to the bay from his apartment. It was a long way for anyone, let alone a restless pre-teen, but the promise of the lake did something to me that you must experience to believe. Past the World of Wheels roller rink and down towards the docks, my dad pointed out deer and birds, and I was never impatient.

When we reached the shore, seagulls were our only company. The beach was dirty, and among the rocks laid bottle caps and soggy napkins, beer bottles from forgotten parties. We were not in a recreational area but close to the shipping yards and could hear the hum of cars crossing the Bong Bridge overhead.

I could easily spot a pretty rock or piece of weathered green glass but lacked the snap of being a good skipper. I always made an effort to launch the rocks just right, and he always attempted to help by telling me I did a great job.

It didn't matter how I did; this was stolen time with my dad without my brothers and sister.

That chilly day years later, when I tried to skip again, the craft was still somewhat lost on me. Schyler and I side-armed rocks at the lake, trying to make them dance. Instead, we thunked one after another into the water and turned to my dad for help.

"Now there's a trick to this," he said carefully selecting a smooth, flat stone and facing the great lake. He placed the rock between his thumb and pointer finger and flicked the rock with the grace of a winning pitcher.

The rock skipped five-six-seven times on the surface before slipping below to the icy depths.

We were in awe. He leaned over and educated us in finding the perfect rock, flicking our fingers just right, throwing it the correct distance from shore.

Practice did not make us perfect or even respectable skippers, so we gradually focused ourselves elsewhere. Schyler grew tired and ran at the water, daring it to soak her shoes. I watched the people riding wacky four-person bikes on the nearby Lakewalk and took pictures.

My dad does not pose for pictures. Until I snuck a picture of him and his homemade bread at Easter time, I hadn't a photo of him to speak of. That day, he posed without objection—his smile radiant.

Though Schyler and I had abandoned them long ago, my dad pitched rock after rock, approaching masterful skips of ten or eleven. And though he seemed old when I was a child, and is only moments from retirement, he was very young that day.

Soon after Schyler's shoes and socks became dripping wet, we decided to head for the car. There was still much to do: cherry pie at Betty's, the cliffs at Split Rock, a rewarding nap back in Superior. The day could have ended right there for me. Somehow I knew the rest of the day, while spectacular, could not compare with the simple art of skipping rocks.

# Wyoming Revival
## by Maggie Delfosse

A couple of hours were all I had, but trying to experience the Grand Tetons in a day hike is ridiculous. The walk was turning out to be just another obligatory been-there-saw-that stop. Even swollen by spring runoff, the waterfall at the end of the trail had been nothing special. Worse, I'd shared it with a group of shrieking teenage girls who, in cutoffs, bright tank tops, and trendy hiking boots, left a dirty scatter of candy wrappers and orange peels littering the wet rocks. Resentfully, I headed back.

Even on a hot day in late May, snow still covered most of the ground. Meltwater following the line of least resistance turned the path into a three-inch-deep creek of crystal over quartz until it reached an edge low enough to let it rush, in streams and mini waterfalls, to the small lakes below. I walked either straddling the path, one foot on the rocks on either side, or squashing though the slush uphill from it, soaking my sneakers.

Above the path, the mountains rise steeply covered in coniferous green. Downhill, the slope falls away clifflike to the base of the uptilt that forms the Grand Tetons where a string of small lakes has collected. A walker turns in and out, alternately passing through sunlight and facing out over the flat land to the east and then moving back into shadowy coves in the mountainside.

On one outward loop, I could see two young men on a dock in the lake just below. Though I was walking in and out of trees, in dark clothes against a shadowed background, and they were in bright sunlight, if they'd looked up they might have seen me. I'm sure they didn't because they were stripping down to go skinny dipping, striped public brown and private white.

The path rounded a knee and I faced in toward the mountain again. From behind me I heard splash … splash … pause … "Oh-h-h Shit!" Young men's big voices breathy with shock cracked the silence and echoed off the rock. They scared a pair of jays into squawking flight. When the trail turned back outward, I could see the dock again, again with two figures on it, but now each one hopping on one foot, one trying to get his jockies back on and the other, without underwear, trying to get a wet foot into the leg of his blue jeans.

I ducked back away from the edge, where I hoped they couldn't hear me, and collapsed onto a rock, laughing, not just because it was banana-peel funny but because I remembered doing exactly the same thing thirty years earlier.

JUST OUT OF HIGH SCHOOL and on the way to college, alone among a crowd of sunbathers and children playing in the water at the edge of the lake on the public beach in Grand Lake, Colorado, I wanted to go swimming. I walked out to the end of the dock, to the side that didn't say, "No swimming this side," and jumped in, feet first. But this wasn't the beach in Maryland I was used to. Where the children were playing, the sun had warmed the shallow water. But the rest of the lake, even in August, remembered being snow on high peaks. Hitting the water was like plunging into a deep blue slushy, and I saw stars. When I finally broke the surface, I sucked in a deep breath of—nothing. At 8,000 feet the air seems thin as vacuum. The swim back to the beach, only a hundred feet or so, felt like a quarter mile, and I fell onto the beach grateful that no one seemed to have noticed.

TIRED AND OUT OF SORTS IN WYOMING, I laughed. To say I laughed until I cried is a cliché. I laughed and then felt like crying. My feet were cold from the slush and getting blisters from the wet; my nose and ears, I could already tell, were going to be painfully sunburned, and I had hours of driving behind me and hours more yet to do. But alone, surrounded by near silence and smelling sun-warmed pine, I could clearly remember the puppy high spirits of jumping without thinking into cold water on a hot day. If I were to go down to the lake and jump in myself, would I be baptized back into enthusiasm again?

I don't know; I didn't try it.

What a shame.

# Murveil Curfew
## by Gina Briefs-Elgin

To reach the castle of the ancient walled town of Murveil de Bezier, you drive up a labyrinth of narrow stone streets, under the flying buttress of the Madonna chapel, and emerge on a broad terrace that overlooks red tile roofs and vineyards in the blue haze. Punch in the key code next to the castle's enormous arched front door, step over the postern threshold, and you're standing in a courtyard garden—two café tables under blue umbrellas, jasmine, pigeons plashing in a stone trough. Look up the circular wall. See way up there, those open shutters and that window box? That's us on the top floor for four nights—my husband Lee, my son Xaver, and me, in Langue d'Oc to celebrate my fiftieth birthday and Xaver's sixteenth.

In this corner of the garden is a dark red door studded with iron knobs, which we open with a six-inch key. We climb round and round up a narrow tower, thirty-five vertiginous stone steps, painted, like the door far below, a dull dark red, clutching at the scratchy sailor rope, thick as a man's wrist, that serves for a banister.

And now we're inside. How lovely! To step from that narrow tower into these high rooms within the width of the castle wall, with their rose toile curtains and chandelier! To look down onto the flagstoned terrace far below where our rented car shines in the afternoon sun, and a child on a bike makes lazy circles. And here we settle, at first for one night, and then for another, then each morning under our breakfast umbrella—"Monsieur, would the rooms be available for yet another night?" Seduced. During the days we explore the countryside, abbeys and wineries. In the early evening we come back to Murveil, eat pizza under sycamore trees on the little plaza in the lower town, drink wine and bottled water "de la Source du Prince Noir," bottled at the Spring of the Black Prince.

The night before we finally leave, Xaver asks if he can take a walk. "Yes, of course," we say. "Take care."

A little before eleven, a conversation begins, something like this. Lee says, "Xaver's not back yet?"

"No. It's not even eleven."

"Well, I don't like him staying out so late in a strange town."

"Hm." I'm sewing a button. I think, It's eleven now, he'll be here any minute.

"It's eleven now. Where is he?"

"He'll be here any minute," I say. We change into night clothes and lie down on the bed. Now it's 11:30.

"Where the hell is he?"

"He's probably thinking of a 12:00 curfew. He'll be in at 12:00. Don't worry."

"Well, I do worry," says Lee.

"It's his last night here. Let him enjoy himself."

Now it's 12:10. I tell Lee (myself), "He's probably given himself a 12:30 curfew."

We're lying side by side on the bed, in the dark, stock still, not touching. The street lamp from the plaza below sends up a little light through the high windows. "He's probably just given himself a 12:30 curfew," I say again, carelessly, but I'm lying stock still in the dark, hardly breathing.

We're not breathing, not rustling the sheet. If we breathe, we'll miss the sound of his footsteps on the stones below.

We're not two people anymore. Lee is not the man who pushed crumbs of bread and chocolate off our map this morning under the breakfast umbrella, smoothing it out to study. I'm not the woman who left the breakfast table and bent over the cool courtyard trough, washing sticky cherry juice from my hands in the sparkling water. We're sonar. We're listening devices, high in this castle wall with the pretty daytime views. Listening for every faintest sound. A distant dog barks once. Ah, I think. Oh, relief. That dog's been wakened by Xaver, hurrying up the narrow cobbled streets of the dark town. A pigeon rustles—no! It's the buzzer of the front door: he's punching in the code. We'll hear his footsteps in the tower in a moment. The sound of a car coming closer, passing under the archway, pulling right up to the castle door—that's got to be Xaver—perhaps some new-found friends are dropping him off.

"He could be dead in a ditch this very moment," says Lee.

At 12:30 sharp, with an unspoken accord, we silently, rapidly dress. Lee says, "We don't even have a photo to show the police."

My insides are like lead. I tell Lee, "It's Friday night. I'll bet it's all lit up down there, he's probably in that café-bar near the patisserie." I can imagine the warm café lights spilling out on the street, people gathered in the soft summer night, laughing and gossiping.

We fling ourselves down the shortcut stone stairs from the terrace to a lower level. We hurry down the narrow winding street, lit wanly by an occasional fluorescent lamp, to the café. It's empty and stone dark, the metal shutter pulled down. Three French teens sit on a step.

"Have you seen our son, sixteen years old, tall? He's blond?"

"*Non, non, on l'a pas vu,*" they say. No, no, we haven't seen him.

"He's probably farther down, at that plaza where the pizzeria is," I tell Lee, tell myself. But in my numb heart the worst has already happened, like a truth I'm postponing. My innards are knotted, not with fear, but with the despair of certainty, of a done deal. We plunge down towards the lower plaza. I prick my ears for music, for voices. Soon we'll hear sounds drifting up from the pizzeria, the smell of pizza, diesel. But under the fluorescent lights, the narrow streets and side streets, street after street, are shuttered and completely abandoned, not a soul, not a dog, not a cat. We reach the pizzeria and it's dark.

Further down, further down.

Maybe he's at that little park with the telephones. Maybe he's calling, calling your mother, a nice surprise.

The streets get wider here, rougher neighborhood where the road from the big town of Bezier feeds in. In a dim alley, two young men are slouching on their *vélos*. I hurry to them. "Have you seen our son? Sixteen, tall. He's blond?"

"He was alone?"

"Yes!"

"*Non,*" they answer. "*On l'a pas vu.*"

What if he's at the *supermarché*, all the way down? What if he's.... But I'm dreaming. Everything is closed stone tight. This is a small French village.

We turn and start walking blindly back uphill.

"I'll run up to our rooms and see if he's there. He's probably back there right now, wondering where we are. We have no way of telling from here." And I run up the narrow winding streets, with their cold bluish lights, up the frightening stone steps of the shortcut—what if I find him here, lying in blood in this hidden place? Through the dark red door, up the dark red steps. Well, of course he'll be up there, already in bed, wondering, "Where are they?"

But our rooms are empty, nothing but the signs of our hasty departure, night things scattered on the bed. I turn off all the lights. I think, all the lights off. This way, we can look some more, and we can look up at our windows and see if he's come back and turned the lights on. Or if the windows stay dark, stay dark.

I pull the heavy door and start slowly down the long circular stair again. What will I tell Lee? What will I tell Lee?

And then I hear the sweetest sounds coming up the windings of the stair, like music—one voice furious, and one sullen teenage voice.

# The Stamp Sands
# by Laura Langer

Every time we got in the car to set off on our long drive to visit my grandparents in the Upper Peninsula of Michigan, each member of my family had a different destination, though we drove the same roads, saw the same cafés in the same small towns, stopped at the same rest stops.

My dad was going home, in the way you go back to where you grew up. We kids were rushing to the old barn that burned down when I was in Puerto Rico in 1973, the fort we could build in the woodpile, my Aunt Ann's horses and chickens, the kittens I dragged around until my mom was sure they were stretched out, a series of unlucky short-lived dogs, the well house, rooms filled with people who came to see my father and his family. My mother, I soon understood, didn't look forward to these trips in the way the rest of us did. Being the in-law, she was the only one of us six not linked by blood to that place and those people, though she loved it fiercely. No wonder my dad liked to mow the two-acre lawn.

My father grew up near the tip of the Upper Peninsula. We drove the 400 miles several times a year to see my grandparents. It wasn't a luxury trip, and the roads were all two-lane then. I don't remember the year we stayed in the small motel where the heat stove turned glowing red in the middle of the night. My dad had to grab it with his bare hands and run outside to dump it in the snow. He was in his shorts. I was sleeping in a drawer.

I do remember asking, every time, whether my grandfather would be there when we arrived. Grandpa Ira was a merchant sailor nine months of the year. When the Great Lakes froze over, he came home. His schedule was a mystery to me. I just hoped every time that he would be there when we arrived.

Before we left home, my father would call his parents and try to give them an estimate of our arrival time. Sometimes we drove straight through, arriving in the quiet hours when even dogs are reluctant to get up and bark at a passing car. Sometimes we left after work and stopped to sleep along the way in some last ditch motel. On those trips, at some point only she understood, between the dinner stop and sunset, my mom would begin her hopeful suggestions. "How about this one?" she'd offer. "Vacancies everywhere," my dad would say. "We'll just go a little further." Invariably the signs started blinking NO soon after that, and we always ended up in a motel with lumpy beds, towels you could see through, and something memorable like sloping floors, holes in the walls, or the famous burning heat stove.

Whatever our ETA, whenever my father expected to be turning off the paved road in the last minutes before we could see the farm, my grandfather sat on the front porch all day while my grandmother was in the kitchen fixing a ham, a turkey, bread, pies.

THE NEXT MORNING, RIGHT AFTER BREAKFAST, I'd head across the fields to my Aunt Ann's, look for deer skulls in the woods, or visit the neighboring farms. I wasn't wild, just free. My brother's favorite thing was to hunt for eggs in Ann's chicken coop. He'd emerge covered in feathers, grinning hugely, a beautiful towheaded boy in a white t-shirt. In the early years my sisters were too little to do much more than toddle around or be passed from one set of arms to another to eat and sleep.

With my father's aunts, uncles, cousins, and old friends stopping by and staying for one meal or three, my grandmother and the other women spent most of their time cooking, setting the table and doing dishes, sometimes talking or playing cards when all the work was done. Before dinner each night my grandmother walked out to the garden with a big scarred stainless steel bowl to pick fresh lettuce for salad. My Aunt Ann was never invited for dinner. I suspected it was the bird's eye maple dresser my grandmother claimed the Olsons had made off with when she wasn't looking. Even at the age of eight I knew there was something more to that story. My mother called it something else.

Some afternoon or morning, we would get into our car and drive out to Gay. Along the neglected paved road, between small, secret towns, we made stops for the waterfall, the sandy beach, and the fishing net winders. If my grandfather went along there was always a chance he'd talk my dad into stopping at some small bar for a shot of Kessler's, "smooth as silk." Finally, a turn off the road into a narrow opening in the trees, no signs, no warnings. There were the stamp sands.

I HAVE BEEN GOING TO THAT STRANGE LANDSCAPE since I was a little girl, but it has never lost its allure for me. The stamp sands are the hidden remains of the copper mines, and meant, to this isolated, beautiful place, as much as the rusted hulks of mine machinery abandoned in Torch Lake. Those copper mines once supported hundreds of families. No one has cleaned them up, or ever will I suspect—not the abandoned machinery, the mine shafts or the stamp sands. In all those visits, they stamped themselves on my memory.

The stamp sands are the residue of the millions of tons of rock and earth the miners dug out of the mountain to get at the copper. My great-grandfather hauled some of that rock up to the cars that took it to the surface. Brutal, literally back-breaking work. By the time I was old enough to notice and remember, his fingers were so gnarled and twisted that he could no longer deal off the bottom of the deck undetected. He hated to lose. He once said to his daughter, my grandmother, that you always knew a child's mother, but no one could say for sure who the father was.

The mines pumped the grey stamp sand for decades—half a mile or more out into the waters of Lake Superior. Hundreds of feet down it goes, solid enough to drive a car across it, right to the water's edge. Nothing grows there. My father told me once that he used to swim in a water-filled hole in the middle of this small grey desert. He said the water was always warm—something you can't say about Lake Superior ever. We walk, look, stare. We climb a small slope and then descend the other side, looking at the water, at the distant green further along the shore, at the uniform grey sand. Then we drive back, turning inland from the big lake—Superior—back towards Torch Lake and the farm.

MY FATHER ONCE TOLD ME that you used to be able to see Torch Lake from the front porch where my grandfather always waited, patiently looking down the road to see a green Pontiac, a white Chevy station wagon, a red Oldsmobile convertible, a blue Cadillac, come round the corner, bringing home his only surviving child and all his grandchildren. My dad thought of buying up that land, clearing and restoring the view. But years passed, my grandfather died in the hospital. We sold the farm and my grandmother moved to a senior apartment building in Lake Linden, where she lived to be ninety-seven-and-a-half, still washing her own dishes, folding the dishcloth carefully to dry. She died on a Wednesday, thirty-six hours after my sister and I left her at the end of a long weekend together.

    I can still see the stamp sands, and the field across the road that used to give a view from the front porch to Torch Lake. I can still feel my grandfather's joy when we arrived, and my grandmother's sorrow when we left.

# The Glasgow Monk
## by Jean Comstock

The first time the monk from Glasgow accosted me was on the corner of Lawnmarket and George IV Bridge in Edinburgh. "I'm from a monastery outside of Glasgow," he began, more timidly than he should have.

Only a few inches taller than I, he was bundled against the damp evening chill with a zipped jacket, heavy gloves, and stocking cap pulled almost to his eyebrows. This didn't look like a monk.

But it was a busy street and, though already long dark in late November, I had no fear of stopping to hear his spiel.

Seeing this, he picked up eagerly, rushing his words before I could change my mind.

"We help young, wayward boys," and he took a step forward to open a homemade book of reformed youths' photos, carefully arranged in plastic sheets.

Would someone running a scam go to that much trouble? Didn't matter. Still in the first glorious days of a six-week trip, I was feeling happy, generous. I knew I was going to give him money. But making him work for it, I asked some innocuous questions first. Afterward, he observed I had a bit of an accent (a remark that floored me every time I heard it). Whenever asked, I first responded that I was from the United States; if people still appeared interested, or looked at me as if I were an idiot, I drilled down to Minnesota.

"Ah, Minnesota." In that melodic brogue, he replied, "I know about Minnesota."

Thinking this would be good for a laugh, I asked congenially what he knew.

"Jesse Ventura," he responded.

I nearly collapsed.

Turns out he had been on a school wrestling team back when Jesse was wearing feather boas more frequently, and they had sometimes watched films of him. Pleased with the encounter and a good story for my friends back home, I happily went on my way.

DAYS PASSED. I TRIED TO FIND my land legs in a town I'd visited before but never by myself and never for a period of weeks. Walking one night by Waverly train station, safe not by virtue of its lighting—having one of the darkest underground entrances I've ever seen—but because of the constantly emerging travelers, a man approached me from the shadows.

"Excuse me, I'm from a monas...," he hesitated, knowing there was something about me.

"Minnesota," I helped him out and dug in my jeans for a pound.

Surprised at another gift, he insisted on giving something back to me and from his over-stuffed backpack came a small, worn book of inspirational sayings. That was the night I found out his name was George, and he found out my name was Jean. The feeling of having a friend, whether he knew it or not, in this town where I knew no one filled me with exhilaration as I walked home.

Over the next two weeks, he gave me a pen, a lighter, a keychain, a candle, and finally, when I had one of everything else, he pressed upon me a stick of Edinburgh rock—long hard candy with the town name magically imprinted throughout.

I felt guilty talking, keeping him from other donors, but he always seemed happy to see me and never in a hurry. In one of our conversations, I learned he alternated between Edinburgh and Glasgow. Knowing I was moving to Glasgow soon, I thought to myself, "I should ask if I can buy him dinner." Just for the conversation. Just for the companionship. Just because I found I was attracted to a Scottish monk. Good heavens!

I GOT BUSY THE FIRST WEEK or so I was in Glasgow. It was many days before I'd had enough sightseeing and decided to go trolling for George at Central Station downtown.

# The Glasgow Monk

I imagined him surprised and delighted at seeing me there, nonchalantly strolling by him, coolly studying the windows of the station's indoor stores. But, halfway down the long row of shops, I began to glance left and right. After twenty minutes, I was moving fast, scanning the crowds in the waiting areas as I loped from ticketing to tracks and back again. Then, dodging food wrappers and stained cups on concrete stairs, I ran from the lower levels to each of the many street entrances.

Finally I stopped. He wasn't there.

As I trudged back to my apartment in the 5:00 twilight, I knew I would never see him again. I had lost him, not realizing until then the depth of the relationship I had built in my head. And I almost wept with disappointment.

Maybe my next journey will be to take a chance. Maybe next time, I'll follow my instincts. Maybe next time, reach out sooner. Maybe. Next time.

# Kiss and Tell: The Tale of a Magical Parade
## by Maureen Breitzmann

*I* once longed for the kiss of an unattractive stranger on the streets of New Orleans. It was an innocent wish. My boyfriend was standing right next to me after all. The man was simply part of a parade that happened upon us while we waited in line for a good meal.

IN THE MOMENTS PRECEDING DARK, we had walked past the crowded blocks surrounding Bourbon Street that gradually trickled into the serene streets leading to K. Paul's restaurant. We went there in anticipation of a well-mixed drink and luxurious eats and found ourselves at the end of a ninety-minute line waiting to get inside. It was not life-ending. In the past, we were known for waiting three hours to ride the latest roller-coaster, so a good plate of food was definitely worth it.

The line snaked down the side of the brick building, with a few windows near the door allowing us to view the lucky diners. The restaurant appeared hearth-like with the patrons as players in a mouthwatering show.

"It's a nice night," my boyfriend Matt offered.

"Yes, it is," I replied, though I was nervous they would reject my jean jacket or lack of sleeves underneath. Despite the wait and our stomachs hollowed from a day of hurricanes, we were put completely at peace in the quiet night.

As other parties combined to get inside faster, we leaned against the cool brick. It was a balmy night, perfect for pants and a light jacket, the ideal respite from a string of long, sticky days.

That's when a parade came passing by.

As if just for us, an Italian-American parade emerged through the twilight of Chartres Street. It was a proud sea of red, white, and green that popped against the seven o'clock sky.

The floats were festive, more exquisite than those of high-school homerooms but by no means pretentious. They carried beautiful dark-haired girls posed in flouncy dresses who waved without moving their bodies but for their petite, cupped hands. It was as if they were music box dolls, with movements strictly dictated and precise. Younger girls threw beads at the crowd.

Boisterous music propelled dance troupes in shiny costumes, and men carried looming masks on twenty-foot poles that miraculously did not get caught in the trees. A local boxer had his very own float, and muscular men dispensed beads bearing boxing gloves.

The stars of the show were a group of Italian men that presented women and girls with a carnation in exchange for a quick kiss. Some men were visions with dark skin and chiseled faces. Others were older, less delicious, but, of course, still sought after for their ninety-nine cent colored flowers.

I watched man after man kiss others on the now-crowded sidewalk, the bunches of flowers in their hands seemingly so large surely they could spare one for me. I did not know why I wanted one so much. Perhaps it was memories of junior high dances when boys would not dance with me to save their lives. Or simply the longing to say I had been kissed by a mysteriously handsome man from the Mediterranean.

The parade was nearing an end. I could feel it because the music of the dance troupes had died to a gentle murmur in the distance, and the streams of beads stopped glinting in the light of the restaurant window before they slapped against the sidewalk.

Finally, a not-so-dashing, not-so-dark-and-dreamy older Italian stopped at my cheek, and I offered it to him. His kiss was fleeting, and had I not known it was coming, I might have dismissed it as a strand of hair tickling my skin. He surrendered the coveted green carnation and disappeared to the next lucky girl. I beamed and tucked the flower into my jacket pocket securely.

As suddenly as the parade began, it ended, and it was finally our turn to go inside.

My attire raised no concerns, and my Blackened Louisiana Drum Fish was perfection. Matt and I shared a Chocolate Hill, a dessert I would long for every day since, and feeling more than full, we left to walk back to our damp hotel room in the quiet night.

It didn't happen then, but long after, that I realized the parade was something special—a glimpse into a world so different from my own. I cannot even name the vast number of nationalities that construct me. I just always say I'm Irish because I am and I think it's neat. But these people did not think being Italian-American was simply neat. They thought it downright important, and they were so proud they stopped traffic on a normally subdued street, and made ninety minutes a flash, a dream, of red, white, and green.

## Roots And Wings
## by Mary Louise Poquette

The oddest things can tie the generations of a family together. In mine, it was not an old rustic cabin, the family farmstead, or Grandma's four-poster; it turned out to be an airplane.

Three summers ago, I had flown out to southern California to see my daughter, Melissa, and my then 6-year-old grandson, Joshua, who live in Camarillo. When I visit them, I am always on the lookout for activities that we can all share, activities, however, that do not include standing in long lines for a few minutes of the manufactured excitement of amusement parks.

One morning, chance brought a gift to me delivered straight to my motel parking lot—a maroon van emblazoned with an airplane logo and the words "Tri-Motor Aviation" lettered in white. A man and a woman were busily loading up equipment, and I had to ask, "Does your business have anything to do with a Tri-Motor Ford?"

"Well, yes," he replied. He and a partner had restored one of the old Ford Tri-Motors, the first commercial passenger airliner, and had brought it down for the Camarillo Air Show. I laughed and replied that I knew all about those planes—my pilot father had logged hundreds of hours in the old Fords during the late 1920's and early 30's, flying first for a short-lived airline out of Tulsa and later as a captain for TWA.

The man introduced himself, Capt. Bud Fuchs—as it turned out, another member of the TWA fraternity—and he asked about my dad.

I told him that my father, despite his daredevil nature, had safely survived the rigors of early flying (perhaps due more to his exceptional skills as a pilot rather than to his good sense), and was still living in Kansas City at the age of 97. We felt an immediate bond. He suggested that I bring Melissa and Joshua to the air show so that we could all go up in the restored plane.

Joshua was ecstatic at the idea of the air show and taking his first airplane ride. Melissa, to whom *Fear of Flying* is not just the title of a book, was not enthusiastic. She hadn't been in an airplane for many years. Nonetheless, we headed down to the airport on the hot, sunny afternoon that turned out to be the future for Joshua and a time warp for me.

I was sent flying back to my childhood, trailing along after my tall, handsome father through the old Municipal Airport in Kansas City.

That airport was my own private playground, like Eloise at the Plaza Hotel, my entree into a grown-up, exciting world, bursting boundaries. I learned geography reading the flight itineraries at each gate. "Pittsburgh, New York, Rome, Athens, Cairo." Mystery. And magic.

It meant the smelly mix, especially on a hot Kansas City summer day, of melting tarmac and aviation fuel. It also meant the thrill of hanging out in the tower with the weather forecasters.

Those good-hearted fellows always made a place for me on a high stool at the map table so I could color on the expired weather maps with—another bit of sheer fascination for me—their special colored pencils with blue lead on one end and red on the other. However did they make the pencils like that? More magic. There's still a stubby one left rolling around at the back of my desk drawer.

And occasionally, in those days of low-tech solutions and more casual regulations, I was even sent, puffed with grown-up pride, to deliver a new weather forecast to a plane down on the runway.

Back at the Camarillo airport, we waited at the edge of the runway to buy our tickets. When I saw the fifty-dollar per person charge, I hesitated. I was going into my second year of unemployment and it seemed like a lot of money. I had the sense, however, that it was, to quote my father, "fish-or-cut-bait" time.

With Joshua dancing wildly around me, I decided to "fish" and pulled out my checkbook. My daughter continued to dither but, finally, not to be left earth-bound by her six-year-old son, also decided on the fishing option and climbed aboard, sweaty-faced and knuckles white.

Captain Bud motioned for us to sit right up behind the cockpit and, much to our surprise, told the other passengers that the three of us were carrying on an old family flying tradition which had started with my father. In fact, we were probably the only family in America, with living members of four generations, all to have flown in one of these historic airplanes.

The deafening thunder of those three powerful Ford engines lifted the grand old plane into the skies. Not exactly a luxury ride, however. The walls were bare wood, and although the windows were large, there was no such thing as air conditioning on that hot day.

In contrast with today's sanitized airline trips, with tiny portholes which allow little connection with the countryside 30,000 feet under an airplane's wings, I felt on this flight that I was truly FLYING.

Suddenly, I saw my dad's early career with new eyes, those pioneering days of aviation when my father as co-pilot found that his duties included not only flying but also passing out sandwiches—and barf bags—to the often traumatized customers. An aviation historian once asked him if he ever had unruly passengers on those early flights. "Naw," he replied. "They were usually too scared to cause any trouble."

As trips go, this was a pretty short one, just up the coast, around Ventura Harbor and back to Camarillo. The sun danced a jig on the water, and we waved out the windows to the sailors beneath us.

Although it might have horrified the FAA, Joshua spent part of the ride in the cockpit with Captain Bud, his face lit up with a huge grin. Even my daughter's face showed a wan smile.

The landing was smooth and light as a feather. As we climbed down out of the plane, I realized that short flight had been significant for each of us.

For Joshua, it was one of the "firsts" in his life, an arrow pointed to the future. For my daughter, it had given her the courage to fly through her fears, bolstering her for the present. For me, it was a connection to my father and to my own past. I thought, "Well, our names may not be Lindbergh, but for us, this was an historic flight."

# It Only Takes a Moment
## by Jean Comstock

When her small hand first touched my back, barely noticeable through a light jacket, I almost thought I had imagined it. As she reached further behind, now to stroke, matching my steps, her dark eyes holding mine with the hint of a smile, I repeated, "No!" more firmly and continued walking. It was when she pressed firmly into the small of my back that I became scared, scared and angry. I swatted her away. And at that moment, Roger spoke softly.

"My wallet's gone."

Then, with a rising sense of panic, "My passport's gone, too!"

The young children, who moments before boisterously surrounded us, had vanished like snowflakes on your tongue. While people continued to scurry down the busy street at mid-afternoon, time had stopped for us.

Moments before we were strolling up the street, squinting in the bright sun, laughing at the perfection of this day, wondering how the photos of the ancient fort would turn out, and gobbling up chocolate-covered, sugary orange slices. While digging into the deep, glossy bag, we hadn't noticed half a dozen children, aged six to twelve, bouncing up before us.

A beautiful young girl held a newspaper at my waist, asking for money.

I shook my head, and said, "No." When they didn't give up but swarmed even closer, I was reminded of children begging in India, gritted my teeth, and moved a little faster. Then the hand on my back, Roger's oddly detached statements, and...it was too late.

For many seconds, we simply stood on the corner, spinning wildly to all sides, desperately hoping to see a child making his way through the crowd with two prizes. Even when it was obvious we could do nothing, we still stood, as if purely by force of will we could reverse time like Superman, taking back the last five minutes, being smarter, being safer, preventing this ruining of our trip.

The Nice police station was gloomy, a warren of dark, narrow rooms that seemed to be dripping with damp. As we tried to explain what had happened, a man behind a bare counter handed us a form. When Roger asked a question, he simply shrugged, not unkindly, and said, "No Anglais." Feeling very alone, we did our best, then watched as he painstakingly typed it all over on a new form, perhaps stalling for the detective who spoke English.

All polite, all respectful, these men were nevertheless weary. The English speaker nodded sadly, saying a group of gypsies had recently camped outside of town and such a thing was to be likely. With unexpected kindness, he sat beside us on a bench in the dreary lobby, quietly explaining why you can never outwit a thief.

"This is his job," he said, "to rob you. The same way you work at your job, he works at his. Everything you buy to protect yourself will not stop him. If you travel enough, one day you will be robbed."

That night we ate quietly, the food we'd previously moaned over, dry and tasteless. Our balcony view of the Mediterranean, the Côte d'Azur, just rocks and water.

By ten the next morning, we were on the train to Marseille and the nearest American embassy. No longer able to be delighted by the spring countryside, we were angry at the French in general. Roger stretched his long legs across the compartment and pretended to be asleep, making an attractive young French woman hop across them and rip the back seam of her skirt.

We were unhappy still when, armed with only the address of a passport photographer, we got lost. A small, elderly man, dapper in a perfect slate gray suit, took the paper without a word, waved us with him, and walked the two blocks to the studio before turning silently and retracing his steps. Later, a young waiter, eager to use his English, heard the story and returned with two complimentary glasses of wine, insisting we not leave with the proverbial bad taste in our mouths. Returning to Nice that evening, new passport in hand, we found we had been charmed by these small actions of strangers. France was again a good place to be.

A bad incident needn't ruin a trip. Have backups in place. Be proactive about fixing what you can. Then accept the rest. Much as you would at home.

And never stop accepting the kindness of strangers.

How easy it is to indict an entire nation when you don't truly know even one person in it. This happens too much in the world today. But in asking for help—from a tired policeman or a dapper old man—we opened ourselves again to the possibility of goodness. And, of course, these people were good. Of course, these people were decent. Of course, these people had nothing against us. We were lucky enough to have the time to find out. We were lucky enough to be open to their kindness. And we found it.

# The BWCA
## by Diane Klein Smith

For me, there is no place on earth like the Boundary Waters Canoe Area on the border of Minnesota and Saskatchewan connecting with all that is real and good in life. The summer of 1974 was hot and dry. Before university classes started, Dave, Mike, Sonja, and I decided to escape the heat and paddle our way in the northern waterways.

WE PUT IN AT THE MOOSE RIVER LANDING. With the smell of pine and birch, the ground soft under our feet, and the spirit of adventure deep within us, we hit the portage. Goodbye telephones, TVs, alarm clocks, schedules, and material stuff. Hello water, wildflowers, and wildlife. From the Moose River, it was an easy paddle downstream to Nina-Moose Lake. We continued down the Nina-Moose River. Here we found a series of sloping rock ledges with gentle rushing water. Ready for a break, we secured our canoes and allowed ourselves time to romp and ride these natural water slides. We reveled in pure and silly glee, the memory of which still brings a smile to my face. We ate a trail lunch—crackers, sausage, cheese, and apples. I'm not sure why, but food always tastes better in the North Woods.

I WANT TO TELL YOU ABOUT THE BEST MEAL I NEVER ATE. We spent our last day paddling and fishing. We caught a northern, several small mouth bass, some croppies, and a perch. We dreamed of the fine dinner we were going to savor that evening. We arrived back at camp just before dusk and were surprised to see that our food packs had been tied high in a tree. Another group of campers had joined us on the island that day. They told us there were bears in the area and advised us to keep our food high. It felt weird to know that someone had been rummaging around our campsite, but we thanked them and headed back to camp.

Dave and Mike went down to the water's edge to clean and prepare the fish. Sonja and I made the campfire and got the rest of the meal ready. Two field mice nibbled on corn meal that was on the picnic table. All of a sudden, the mice scampered off the table into the woods. We chuckled and wondered what had prompted their quick departure. That was when we heard a rumbling behind us, followed by a loud, "Grrrrrrr!" We stopped what we were doing, looked at each other, and then slowly turned our heads to look at what we had heard. There, no more than twelve feet behind us, sat an enormous bear.

Simultaneously we arose, walked to the other side of the table, and ran to the water to inform Dave and Mike of our camp visitor. They weren't concerned and informed us that the bear was probably more afraid of us. They instructed us to bang pots and pans and fan the fire, certain this would convince the bear to leave. So, we returned to bang the pots and pans and fan the fire until it was blazing. These actions made no impression upon the bear who continued to sit, stare, and snarl at us.

The guys returned. I wondered how they remained so calm, but they were confident the bear would leave. After putting the fish on the fire, the guys began beating on the pots and pans and chiding the bear with humorous slurs. They said things like, "Hey, go find your own fish, you big, lazy bear." And, "You're so ugly your mother would have to tie pork chops around your neck to get the other bears to play with you." The bear did not find their remarks amusing. It let out a huge rumble. It was then we saw two small cubs peering from behind the bear. At this point, the guys joined us on the other side of the table yelling, "Grab the gear and head for the water!"

You never saw four people fly so fast. We lifted the tents, bags and all, and threw them into the bottom of the canoes and headed out into the water. In the dark of the night, we sat very still wondering what to do next. The bear did not move either. We finally paddled to another island and set up our tents and bags. Our dinner that evening consisted of one candy bar, some leftover gorp, and an apple. As we tucked ourselves into our bags, we heard the bear give out an enormous howl. Mike said, "I hope that bear got a bone stuck in its throat." Speaking for myself, I was glad the bear was content to feast on our gourmet fish and wild rice instead of us!

We returned to the scene of the crime the next morning. The bears had licked our pots and pans clean. They had even bitten holes through the frying pan. We packed the remaining gear and began our paddle back to civilization.

Thirty years have passed since we shared our meal with the bear family. We laugh harder with each retelling of the story, remembering our fear, grateful for life. The BWCA is an amazing place. However briefly you may travel through its ancient waterways, the experience leaves you with satisfying memories and makes you yearn for more.

## The Best Sights in London: Traveling With Daughters
### by Karen Ackerman

Would there be drug-sniffing dogs at Customs? I worried the entire eight and a half hours from London to Minneapolis. Longer, if you count the hours after I checked my bag and regretted not throwing the stuff away. I had wrapped it in paper and then bound it tightly in layers of plastic. Still the weedy odor was distinctive and those dogs knew their business. All I could think was, "Will they let me explain, or will they cuff me, print me, and take my mug shot before I can say 'Bob's your uncle,' or 'It's only hair dye.'"

It was only hair dye—honest! And, to quickly allay any anxiety you might be feeling, the airport beagles were off on another case. I slipped through Customs.

This near-brush with the law began when my oldest daughter, Miriam, who had just completed her junior year of college abroad, asked if she could stay in London for the summer, promising, of course, to keep learning, to make more connections, etc. I said sure and immediately began planning my trip. I've never understood why parents whose children study outside the U.S. feel they, too, must go, but before June was out my youngest daughter, Tovah, and I were on a plane to Gatwick.

Throughout May and the first half of June I laid out the itinerary: one day for Hampstead Heath, Highgate Cemetery, and the famous Rembrandt self-portrait at Kenwood House, another for the Inns of Court, Black Friar's Pub, and Temple Church where Knights Templar recline at one's feet. Evenings would be for theater: *Les Miserables*, some fringe, and perhaps the new Andrew Lloyd Webber. My plan did not include watching BBC TV and eating deli food in bed while marinating my face in a decoction of seaweed and dirt.

On our first morning in London, after a quick juice and coffee, we headed for the Victoria and Albert Museum and then off to Harrods. Our second morning found us back at the V&A before checking out the shops on King Street. A cloud was forming over my head. What about Wren's churches? When were we going to Hampstead Heath? By the third day we had made it as far as Kensington High Street, London's junior's department. I heard thunder between my ears but kept my mouth shut. "Don't be such an old stick," I said to myself. "The girls are having fun." We strolled on, landing eventually in LUSH. LUSH is a chain of cosmetic stores where all products are natural: blocks of Coalface and Fresh Farmacy; tiny tubs of Dream Cream, Ultra Bland, and The Sacred Truth; barrels of Bath Ballistics and Bubble Bar Slices. Friendly young people answered our questions politely and thoroughly, explaining the benefits of odd globs of creams and cleansers.

Instead of theater that night, we headed back to our small room off Gloucester Road, our arms filled with bags of stuff. While Tovah channel surfed, landing on a BBC mystery, Miriam hacked at the cube of herbs and henna called Caca Rouge (French for Red Poo) and stirred it into a warm, mahogany paste. I spread the bed with our supper of Chicken Korma and Tikka Masala from the deli at Waitrose Grocery. Our room smelled like an Indian bazaar. Imagining themselves as enchanting redheads, the girls slathered their hair in poo and wrapped their heads in plastic wrap. All three of us smeared Love Lettuce over our faces and waited to be reborn.

I'll make this short. My face, unmasked, looked clean but no younger. Tovah's dark brown hair, after an hour and a half under wraps, was still dark brown with a few copper strands. But Miriam's hair—oh my. Miriam's hair shone sunset orange. Tovah sat at the bottom of the bed, motionless. I bit my bottom lip. "What do you think?" I asked finally. Miriam looked at herself in the mirror and shrugged, fluffed her hair, and shrugged again. "I don't think I'll need the rest. You can take it home." But she was smiling.

Every time I travel I forget and need to be hit upside the head with a chunk of poo before I remember. Planning a trip is fun. I might even say it's half the fun. I love it that much. But the plan is not the point. The real journey often begins when the plan unravels. I planned to see what the guidebooks touted. I did not expect to be stopped by the sight of my own children.

We eventually made it to Highgate Cemetery and Hampstead Heath. We saw *Les Mis* and something by Pinter. Temple Church was closed for an afternoon lecture we weren't invited to (bless them), but we did have lunch at Black Friar's. We sat beneath the low vaulted ceiling on velvet cushions, surrounded by brown and gold mosaics. I looked across the table through sepia light. Tovah raised her head and smiled lightly, as beautiful and timeless as any Rembrandt canvas. Beside her, Miriam sat looking down at the menu, her long, brilliant hair falling forward, like orange silk. What had I been thinking? Here, in front of me, sat the best sights in London.

# Voodoo
## by Jane Congdon

*P*ockets of primitive religion still exist in the United States, deep and dark and rhythmic as a heartbeat. We had a woman in Glen Ferris who used to wring chickens' necks. As a child I had seen this, though I did not know the reason for it. The pull of voodoo, with its dangerous mysteries, had always been as irresistible as a spell. I had seen Angel Heart, but this was not the movies. Now, in the belly of superstition and enchantment—the Louisiana Bayou Country—I would see firsthand secrets of the chicken-bleeding, gyrating, skeleton-clacking, curse-filled voodoo religion.

I was in New Orleans on a business trip. I'd come a day early just for this, a two-hour cemetery and voodoo tour. What would it be like to visit a voodoo shop? Would I be marked as soon as I crossed the threshold? Cursed with the evil eye? Made into a doll? Did they cater to a certain few, or could I walk in and buy a potion off the shelf? I pictured powders, roots, ground-up animal parts: cat claws, frog skin, bird bones; a curtain at the back where clerks slipped into another world.

On Sunday morning, we met our guide outside a café on Royal Street. We set out walking in ninety degree heat, past restaurants, shops, and pastel houses whose doorways opened onto the street. A horn played slow jazz in the background. We saw flower boxes and balconies, gardens and gates, courtyards and churches.

St. Louis Cemetery No. 1 is the burial place of the famous voodoo priestess,

Marie Laveau. The cemetery is a walled maze, unsafe at night, where superstition lingers. Patrons had placed small gifts—a candle, a vase of flowers—at the base of Marie Laveau's tomb to stay in favor.

In New Orleans, the dead are buried above ground; of course, we all know that some come back. *Dawn of the Dead*. In my mind I saw Marie Laveau and her worshippers, men lean and skin shining, women with wrapped heads. I daydreamed images of snakes, people writhing to drumbeats in the night and sending themselves into trances going out of their heads. We were about to meet one.

We cut through Congo Square, where in some past life people of color had performed their sensual dances in public. We passed a statue of Louis Armstrong and continued on to East Rampart Street, angling toward a tiny store with lace-curtained windows. This would be the authentic voodoo temple where we were to have an audience with Priestess Miriam. Our guide warned us that the priestess was a non-linear speaker, and that we might be back home before we truly got her message. I wondered about Priestess Miriam's origins: What language would she speak? Would she chant? Worship? Stage a sacrifice?

In the store, we waited while our guide went down a corridor and talked low to a woman in an orange dress. The store clerk was not Baron Samedi, fresh from the Islands in his black top hat, but a middle-aged man wearing a short-sleeved shirt. He was cordial, but not overly interested in another tour group passing through. We got the signal to come ahead, filing into a dim little room with a linoleum floor. This was the moment.

I sat on the floor with the others and looked around. The temple was full of stuff: wall hangings, pottery, upright figures, little objects, and a feeling of dust. No serpents, no goats, no pins in dolls. In came the woman in the orange dress. Dark, with close-cropped hair, she was Priestess Miriam.

She stood before us, smiled down, and delivered fifteen minutes of benevolent advice. She was English-speaking but not astute. We in the head-nodding front row did not give this away. Priestess Miriam's logic cut a crooked path as she told us how to weed the "crap" grass out of our lives. My mind was screaming the unanswered question: What happens here? Did Priestess Miriam, in another guise, squeeze into this room with her subjects late at night, keening and swaying and losing track of time? This was what we all wanted to know.

What we found out was that before coming to New Orleans, Priestess Miriam had worked at a hospital in Chicago. She had been married, and her husband had passed away two years before. Ordinary. Normal. No bones or feathers, no bowls of blood. Not a word or glimpse of the strange world in which she was held on high.

In the teahouse next door, our tour guide nursed a cold drink while a couple monopolized her with questions about the city. A young man lazed nearby. Two others talked by the cash register. I clung to them all with my eyes, trying to see beyond the specialty drinks and biscotti. Everything was normal, ordinary, and harmless. The strangest sight of the day was an ad on the wall for Voo Brew in which a grinning black man held up a glass as if making a toast, inviting us to "Drink an Iced Priestess Miriam." And I did. "Do you think she's in you?" my son would ask later. I didn't know. This was not the movies.

# Lauri
## by Brenda Wolfe

*I* wouldn't describe her as a good roommate. I wouldn't call her a friend. In fact, I didn't particularly like her, and I barely knew her. Twenty-five years ago, we shared a house for three months when we were college students.

LAURI ANSWERED AN AD I HAD PLACED at the student housing office for two roommates. She and her friend Victoria moved in their sparse belongings in November, taking the upstairs bedrooms. I had the bedroom on the first floor.

Victoria, a tall, angular, freckled redhead with a set jaw worked as a restaurant manager in a pizza joint. Her boyfriend was in France studying to be a chef at Cordon Bleu. Lauri was studying at the University. She was chubby-cheeked and curvaceous, with a thick mane of auburn-colored hair. She wasn't more than five feet tall and had a big smile to go with her giggle.

The kitchen of the house was a bright room, painted a pale green. Against the kitchen windows was an *I Love Lucy* chrome-trimmed, Formica table with matching flecked pastel, vinyl chairs. Each chair back had a big button and was edged with silver-colored, decorative furniture tacks.

Lauri and I had been roommates for about two months when we finally sat down together for tea at the kitchen table on a bright late December afternoon. We had the typical getting-to-know-you conversation as college students do.

When you are young, your experiences are limited, and you can cover a lot of superficial ground fast. Our baggage was still quite light. We exchanged information. Lauri was from Racine, Wisconsin. I grew up in Milwaukee. We were both twenty-one. We were both Jewish. I can't remember what her major was—anthropology or psychology perhaps. I think I had decided on majoring in English Literature by then.

We turned to talking about our families. "My mother is from Germany," I said.

Lauri perked up and said, "My father is from Germany." Thus began the inevitable conversation of first generation Jewish-Americans. The foremost question being, what happened to your family during the war?

"Where is your mother from in Germany?" Lauri asked.

"Frankfurt," I responded. Her eyes widened.

"My father is from Frankfurt, too. When did your mother come to America?" Lauri asked.

"When she was eighteen—in 1941. She was on the last boat of Jews to leave Germany. How about your father?" I asked.

Our eyes locked. Lauri nearly shouted, "1941. He was on that ship, too." Incredulous at the coincidence, we were silent for a moment.

We pondered over whether or not they actually knew each other. We agreed that if my mother and her father didn't know each other personally, our families had surely been acquainted in Frankfurt. The Jewish community wasn't that large there, especially by 1941.

Our parents were only slightly younger than we were when they were forced to immigrate to wherever they could. What were the odds that two daughters of the few remaining Frankfurt Jews running for their lives would sit across the kitchen table forty years later in Minneapolis, in America, on a sunny winter afternoon? We had survived our parents' journey after all. Lauri and I had our whole lives ahead of us, and we knew it. Lauri and I were astoundingly lucky, and we knew it. Our bond, our family history commonality didn't draw us any closer. We never discussed our connection again.

Later in my life I would meet other Jewish people my age and older who were obsessed with the Holocaust, obsessed with being children of survivors, obsessed with how this event, this persecution not experienced, affected, informed, and shaped their lives. Lauri and I were just glad to be young and alive.

Lauri and Victoria moved out a month later. I was actually glad to see them go. They were always borrowing my stuff and leaving a mess. I never saw Lauri again.

# Dachau
## by Virginia A Broich

Dachau was not part of our Alpine Adventure tour in 2000. My eighty-four-year-old mother and I had signed up for a trip with a group of fifty people from her church to go to Oberammergau, Germany, where the Passion Play is reenacted every ten years. Our tour was to take us first to Munich, Germany, then Oberammergau, and finally to cities in Austria, Liechtenstein, Switzerland, and back to Germany.

Mother and I met at her home in South Jersey. On the day of departure, one of my sisters drove us over to the church. We boarded a bus with the group for the Newark Airport and flew out of Newark to Munich, where we met our German guide who moderated our experiences throughout our trip in an air-conditioned bus.

Settling down in Munich for three days, we began our first round of tours. Among the places we bussed to was the ornate Nymphenberg Palace. As I walked through the high-ceilinged rooms and hallways of the Palace, I lingered in one hallway where I noticed a bucolic painting hanging high above me. The serenity of the countryside, the lone house, the washed-out colors blending in greens and browns, the vast area of undeveloped land, gave the painting a postcard-from-the-past quality. My eyes searched for the name of the painting. A one-word plaque attached to the top of the frame of the painting identified the place simply as "Dachau." I thought how unbelievably serene this painting was, given the horror of the concentration camp which would house Holocaust victims on that very land a century later. I could not get this tranquil image out of my mind as our group prepared to go to the site of present-day Dachau the following day.

As I remember, our guide told our group he could get tickets to see Dachau, which is about twenty miles outside Munich, and asked us if we wanted to go. Although Mother and I were a little dubious about spending money to see a concentration camp on what was supposed to be more or less a pleasure trip, we thought it would be worthwhile and decided to pay the extra money.

On the road to Dachau, the city where the first concentration camp was established by Hitler for political prisoners on March 20, 1933, our German guide gave us a somewhat apologetic version of how Germans treated their prisoners. He related that Germans were mentally, not physically, torturing the people, as if that made a difference. If a prisoner tried to escape, everyone in the camp stood in the open area for a day and a half without food and water. "This is not physical?" I thought. When he ended his lecture our guide told us, "Go to the museum and see what they expose."

ONE THING MOTHER AND I HATE ABOUT GUIDED TOURS is that we have to follow someone else's schedule. Sometimes, we concede, this is a good thing, but our minds are not always curious about the same things other people are fascinated by. This was the case for me in Dachau. I had taught about the Holocaust in my Humanities class. One of my students won first place at the Minnesota History Day Competition with a paper he'd written on the Holocaust. I had met and talked with a Holocaust survivor from the Twin Cities who showed me his camp identification number carved into his arm. And, I had visited the Holocaust Museum in Washington, D.C. In my mind I felt I had a fairly good background of the Holocaust. So, when we were told that the first part of our forty-five minute visit to Dachau was a video on the history of the Holocaust, I left my mother with the video group to explore the camp on my own.

ONCE OUTSIDE THE BUILDING THAT HOUSED THE VIDEO AREA and museum, I became obsessed with finding the crematoriums so I could photograph them. I had no idea where they were or what to look for. Yes, I could have read the map more carefully at the entrance to the camp, but my randomness had kicked in, and I was off and running.

On my search I stopped long enough to walk through the reconstructed barracks built on the grounds. All informational signs were in German, of course, so I had to guess at some of the meaning. Seeing the ten toilets in one room and the wooden bunks in another were powerful nonverbal images. As I glanced through the window of the barracks, I thought I saw the crematoriums and took a photo of what looked like an oven in the distance. Once out the door of the barracks, I walked past the expansive, grassy area which once housed about sixteen barracks only to discover that the building I had photographed was the Jewish Memorial.

Our guide had said we'd only be at Dachau for forty-five minutes. Time was running out. I had not found the crematoriums. In and out of the Catholic and Lutheran memorials and a Russian Orthodox Chapel, through the Church of the Reconciliation, across the grassy trenches bounded by a semblance of barbed wire which bordered a small forested area. I looked up and saw the smoke stacks of a building. Here were the crematoriums. I took my photo and stood transfixed in front of the old canvas stretcher inside the oven.

I raced back to the bus where I found my mother and some of the group waiting. We compared notes and discussed what we'd seen as our bus drove us to our hotel in Munich.

Back at our hotel, I was exhausted from my walk. The experiences of the day had drained me both physically and mentally. In the wake of all this, I realized I had made a personal, unplanned pilgrimage. Like the land in the painting, I, too, had been changed.

# Birthdays and Umbrellas
## by Susan Slater Blythe

OCTOBER 4, 1948

Birthdays were big deals at my house. The early ones I can remember from the family album; Grandma and Grandpa Slater crouched on the floor while I opened the colorful packages piled around me. The pictures are in black and white but sometimes, just briefly, they flash on the page almost as if they really were in color and the years have faded them into darker shades of grey. The look captured on my face is one of puzzlement, as if I cannot understand why this is happening, but the adults around me radiate warmth, anticipation, and a gleam of knowing a secret just before it happens.

As I grew older the circle of adults was replaced by girls my own age in pinafores and patent-leather slippers, and my look changed to haughty importance as if I knew the secret and no one else did. The beginnings of the quest to be in charge of everything, even my own celebrations. But, even these later pictures were filled with balloons, streamers, and innocence born of birthdays.

Although I can still remember some of the most special parties and presents, especially the ones that signaled a passing from one plateau to another—a gold picture locket, my birthstone ring, the first pair of slightly high heels—the present I remember the most is not pictured in the albums.

It arrived in October on a clear crisp day. The sky was blue, as bright as the birthstone ring I would unwrap years later, with dollops of clouds traveling across a sapphire sea. As I sat with my mother on the damp steps of our front porch, I remember a brilliant red oak leaf blowing across my shoe as I waited for my mother to cut the twine on the brown package. As she fumbled with the paring knife she mumbled something about, "Oh, your Aunt Agnes can never do anything on time." My Aunt Agnes was married to my mother's brother and somehow that made her my aunt—instead of a regular aunt like Aunt Jane who was everybody's aunt. I didn't understand it. I was just wishing Mom would hurry so I could see what was inside the long funny package addressed to me.

When the string was finally cut and the paper ripped from the box and the top taken off, hidden in the folds of white tissue was a shiny red umbrella just my size with an upside-down Mickey Mouse head for the handle. It was the best umbrella I had ever seen.

All morning, hoping those white clouds were rain clouds, I marched up and down the sidewalk with the Mickey Mouse head, right side up this time, in my hand poking the umbrella's stem through the cracks and leaves, eying the sky overhead. By lunch time it still hadn't rained, so when I went in to eat my dumb old tomato soup and grilled cheese sandwich, I didn't really taste it because I kept thinking I heard thunder, and I didn't want to miss it by being told it was too stormy to go out again by my mother who was always worried about those things.

By the time I finally got back outside, it still hadn't rained, and I must have only imagined the thunder because it was getting hot. It wasn't going to rain! But maybe it didn't really matter. Maybe, instead of sending me a rain umbrella for my birthday, my Aunt Agnes had sent me an umbrella like the ones I remembered in pictures at Aunt Jane's house when she and my grandmother Slater were little girls. Just maybe, this umbrella was made for sun.

So I tried it out. It was a sun umbrella! I strolled, I hopped, I skipped up and down, back and forth in front of the hill next to the steps fading to the front porch of my house. Women in cars, sitting next to their husbands, smiled at me as they drove by. I felt just like a princess.

Just then, right after the lady who waved at me in the grey car drove out of sight, a group of boys heading back up Hartzel Avenue to school rounded the corner laughing. Loudly they pushed past me and not one of them asked to see my umbrella. Not even Billy Thomas who always chanted as I skipped up the walk, "Soo-san-jay-ane-cider, Soo-san-jay-ane-cider, Soo-san-jay-ane-cider."

That was the day I realized, a few days after my fourth birthday, boys never notice the important stuff.

# Lost in Pepper Town
## by Laura Langer

We could see the hotel. We just couldn't get there. It's a four-story, half-timbered former abbey set on a hill in a relatively small town, so it wasn't like it was hard to see from any number of locations within Caen. For the first forty-five minutes, as we drove an endless circle of one-way streets, it was funny. The second forty-five minutes turned increasingly grim. We once got within a half block but couldn't see any parking. I drove on, we were hopeful, but it wasn't to be.

MY SISTER AND I WERE TREATING MY NIECE to a graduation trip in France and England with my mother. After a few days in Paris, we headed off to Normandy to see a tiny slice of this beautiful area, visit Omaha Beach, and find my sister's boyfriend's uncle's grave in the American Cemetery. Paris had been beautiful, but it was difficult to get everyone in synch, and being the only French speaker, and having planned the trip, I was feeling the pressure.

Caen is the largest town near Operation Overlord, *les Plages du Débarquement*, the D-Day beaches. We nearly missed the train from Paris, because we were inattentively standing one very empty platform away. It was the first time I'd seen my mother run in at least five years. The conductor pulled her up the last step, and we all settled in for a few hours.

THE FIRST DIFFICULTY IN CAEN AROSE when it appeared that all the bus tours of the Operation Overlord area were five- or six-hour trips. By noon neither my mother nor my niece had broken a smile, and they vetoed the bus trip. So we two cheerful ones (complaining all the way) took a cab back to the train station area where we rented a Renault Clio. After a long explanation in French of the finer points of the rental contract, we walked outside to find our little Clio. My sister looked in the window and said, "I hope you drive a stick shift." My somewhat rusty standard transmission skills quickly picked up but I would still manage to stall the car not once, not twice, but three times in front of the man collecting money at the parking lot at Avranches. As we pulled away—a little unsteadily—from the Avis office, we were laughing.

We picked up my niece and my mother at the hotel and headed off for the local tourist office for information on self-guided tours. The rather odd French woman there told us there were no guidebooks in English because someone else had neglected to order them, clearly not her error. I already had mine in French and Spanish, but an English guidebook was a must for the rest of the group. The tourist office woman turned to us impatiently and said we should just take the German one because "the pictures are all the same." Well, what can a person say to that? Into the car, all four laughing at last, we set out for the American Cemetery.

The mood picked up in the car as we passed what seemed like mile-long fields of rapeseed in bloom—carpets of yellow flowers like nothing I've ever seen. When the *Pain 16h* appeared on a handwritten sign by the side of the road, faces actually lit up and we pulled quickly off the road to fortify ourselves with a baguette and some sweet treats before moving on.

We stopped briefly at the artificial harbor site at Avranches—site of the three-time stall—and arrived at the American Cemetery just after closing. Despite clearly-marked signs about the closed cemetery, in a burst of optimism we followed some other beleaguered tourists along a road which turned out to lead down to Omaha Beach for our first look at the famous landing spot. Then we got back in the car and headed for Caen, eager for supper, and an early night.

THE FIRST TIME WE PASSED THE HOTEL WE LAUGHED. The second time we couldn't get that close, but we still chuckled. We joked past the daffodils in front of the city hall, admired the church, and laughed again at the idea of "just take the German book—the pictures are the same" as we passed the tourist information office for the third time. The hotel hove into view again, and all of us desperately searched for that one, crucial, hidden turn we needed to take to end up in front of the hotel. Back past the daffodils, the church, around a new area of town with residential neighborhoods, and down past the pedestrian areas where once again we knew how to walk to the hotel but couldn't drive there. "There it is," my sister said. "I hate Pepper Town." From that moment on Caen, not cayenne, became Pepper Town for my sister. Brief, bitter grunts of assent issued from all, then more despairing silence. Past the high school for the fourth time, around the daffodil curve, big gray church, residential neighborhood, tourist office, and another view of the hotel. An offer from me, the driver, to let everyone out to walk to the in-view hotel and I'd fend for myself with the car. No, all for one and one for all. More silence. Around the back of the hotel, but can't turn left here because it's one way the other way. Daffodils, church, post office, tourist office, and finally, finally the special little turn around the corner off the main road and I stop the car in front of the hotel. I refuse to put the car in gear again until they all get out.

TOMORROW, IN "PEPPER TOWN," WE WILL FIND THE COIN my sister wants to buy for her boyfriend. I will have a long conversation in French with the *patronne* of a chocolate and tea shop called Chocolaté, and she will say when she hears we have been to the Cimitière Americain, "Such a beautiful place, but so sad." ["*C'est très joli, mais très triste.*"] My mother will still be limping along on blistered feet, and I will be looking forward to being in a country where all four of us speak the language. We will take two more trains, almost miss the Eurostar to London, forget our patiently packed boxes of chocolate on the train, and my niece will thank me sweetly for everything I have done to plan this trip, making me as happy as I ever could have asked. I will step into the rainy air of London and start my love affair with England. But that will be tomorrow. Tonight, after ninety minutes of seeing the same damn daffodils, the same ugly church, and remembering the same, singularly sullen tourist office lady with the German guidebook—I will find a parking spot a block and a half away.

# Strolling with Mr. Zhue
# by Virginia A. Broich

Sweet-smelling scent of sandalwood emanated from the box. My mind wandered, as it often does, to another place and time. I land on solid ground in Hangzhou, China, the capital city of the Song Dynasty from 1127-1279 A.D. The Song Dynasty was characterized by the rise of a new wealthy group of commoners, the mercantile class.

The person who enlightened me about the modern merchant class in Hangzhou still lives there. At the time I met him, Mr. Zhue was the Dean of Students at the Hangzhou Foreign Language School. It was 1988, the year before Tiananmen. I was part of a group of teachers on an educational tour of eastern China. At the time, "free talk" was not all-pervasive. It occurred only in informal settings, so we deferred questions to the leaders of the groups at the school. We were not allowed to ask questions without an intermediary. The unofficial leaders of the Chinese and U.S. groups were male. After completing the protocol, Mr. Zhue asked us if we wanted to tour Hangzhou on foot for three hours. I jumped at the chance.

Mr. Zhue, a born teacher, was in his element as he escorted a robust, curious group on our walk. He was a man of slight stature, with glasses, black hair, and brown eyes that twinkled when he joked with us. With his surprisingly good sense of humor, he untiringly walked us through a failing supermarket, the free market, streets teeming with taxis and what must have been thousands of bicycles. He pointed to street merchants selling frogs, watermelon, peaches, and other fresh produce. Commerce and business protocol, Mr. Zhue seemed to know everything. Fluent in Chinese and English, he felt at ease with both our group and the group he worked with at the school.

As we began our stroll around the city, the formality and protocol that permeated the school setting soon disappeared. Out on the streets of Hangzhou, I did not have to bow to custom. Mr. Zhue and I were equals.

Walking down the sidewalk, Mr. Zhue lit up a cigarette. For our first lesson he discussed the significance of cigarettes when conducting business in China.

"Cigarettes are both a gift and a communication tool," he explained. "I send you cigarettes first and then we start to talk." Someone who received Marlboro cigarettes would be "a very high person." Hangzhou cigarettes were "middle." If you were sent West Lake cigarettes, that is the lowest, Mr. Zhue commented. In 1988, buying Marlboro cigarettes from a street merchant cost 7 yuan or almost $2.00.

One of the members of our group asked Mr. Zhue if Chinese people knew how bad cigarettes were for them.

Mr. Zhue shouted, "They know! They know! They know!"

"They are like our people. They know; they smoke," I chimed in.

Mr. Zhue admitted he was a heavy smoker, which probably accounted for his thin frame.

"In my office people come frequently to ask you something. Then they send cigarettes. You cannot refuse. Sometimes they will have some bad opinions if you refuse. Then they will think you don't want to do things for them."

I asked what brand of cigarettes he smoked.

"I smoke everything," he replied.

Some of us in the group wanted to bring back items for our classrooms. I had an idea of something I wanted to buy, but not a touristy thing. I was determined to go home with some authentic Chinese music. Accommodating our group, Mr. Zhue steered us into a small, hole-in-the-wall store where two young people stood behind a counter.

In English I told Mr. Zhue what I wanted to buy—classical Chinese music, which usually means music popular during the Tang Dynasty and heard in some hotels that catered to overseas Chinese. I also wanted some music of popular Chinese artists that Chinese teenagers enjoyed listening to. He translated my request into Chinese, but the two young people behind the counter began chanting in English, "Michael Jackson, Michael Jackson." What a shock! Michael Jackson had infiltrated China!

Not giving up, I restated my request to Mr. Zhue. I could see how he struggled to gain the young merchants' understanding that this teacher from the United States did not want to buy a Michael Jackson tape. She wanted to bring some Chinese culture home to her students. Finally, they showed some tapes to Mr. Zhue, and he suggested which tapes would be best. I bought the coveted tapes, and we strolled out onto the sidewalk.

After walking a short way, we stopped in front of the free market, a combination of the Farmers' Markets in Minneapolis and St. Paul and the Reading Terminal in Philadelphia, where merchant-farmers from surrounding areas brought meat and produce to sell. The cavernous market area was open on either end, no sign of a door. Huge windows, however, provided protection and light from the sides of the building. Two long aisles with vendors on each side extended from one end of the building to the other. Inside, I saw customers shopping freely.

As we entered the market, we immediately heard the clamor of commerce. I was intrigued by the words "free market." Obviously, the merchants here were selling produce and meat.

"Was it really free?" I naively asked Mr. Zhue.

"Free to negotiate a price," he responded. He added that there was a price for which you could not go "over the line." Laughingly, he remarked that if we (the foreigners) were to come and try to buy something at the market, "they will stick you."

We ambled by the fresh produce, very important to the Chinese people, according to Mr. Zhue. The Chinese liked to buy their produce in "one hour," he joked. "Right out of the ground." That was the main reason he believed that supermarkets would never work in China. "It seems the supermarket is not viable in China," he observed. He added that the Chinese did not have a lot of packing plant facilities to keep produce fresh.

Searching for foods I could identify with, I noted the eggplant shaped like a cucumber, very different from my fat, oval Minnesota-grown eggplant. We walked past merchants selling onions, peas, roots, green peppers, garlic, tomatoes, Chinese sausage, and unappetizing-looking large, brown lumps Mr. Zhue called "beef." The beef looked more like cow pies, I mused to myself. The meat was not kept in cases nor was it refrigerated. A few flies flew around the meat. I was okay with the produce not being kept cool and fresh in cases, but the meat?

Meat came in the forms of soft shell turtles and eels, which seemed to be popular but expensive. Mr. Zhue told us that soft shell turtles were "very expensive" because "they can cure cancer." I wondered what the reasoning was behind this claim. He told us these turtles contain lots of protein, "especially on the soft side." Smaller eels were not as expensive as the larger ones. To prepare an eel, the cook must first cut it into small pieces. The eel was combined with ginger or "very fresh" onions, Mr. Zhue told us.

As we came down the aisle to the stall where eels were being sold, I stopped. There were at least twenty live eels wiggling on a makeshift wooden countertop. I was fascinated by their motions that, until now, I had only observed on the Discovery Channel and in zoos. Beside me, I noticed a Chinese woman was attempting to buy a live eel and had dropped it on the cement floor. Impulsively, I dropped the small tape recorder I'd been using to record Mr. Zhue's comments and the sounds of the market and jumped in to help. I grabbed the eel so the woman could put the wiggling animal into her burlap sack. At that point, I experienced firsthand the adage, "Slippery as an eel." I, too, dropped the eel before I could plunge it wiggling deep into the sack. A young man came out of nowhere to assist us. Since I spoke no Chinese and he spoke no English, we were reduced to hand signals. He carefully picked up the eel between his two fingers and motioned to me as if to say politely, "That's how it's done." I bowed to thank him. That's all I could think of to do. He bowed and wandered away to another part of the market. Soon our group left the market, its chatter, and its now familiar smells.

IN MY MARKET EXPERIENCE I HAD BEEN INTRODUCED to an important side of Chinese culture. I realized that the food we call "Chinese" in the United States is not what the average Chinese person eats. The images of the marketplace and Mr. Zhue are indelibly etched in my mind, even after sixteen years.

# Zywiec
# by Marla Kapperud

It was supposed to be so simple: board the train in Bratislava at two o'clock p.m., arrive in Krakow about midnight. I was assured the train was direct by the busy ticket agent. During my two hour wait for the train, I try calling a taxi driver in Krakow, a man whose name was given to me by a friend who travels frequently to Poland. For reasons I don't understand, I can't make the connection and I can't figure out what I'm doing wrong. After running out of coins and time, I board the train.

A FEW HOURS INTO MY JOURNEY, I BEGIN TO WORRY. Will I be able to find a cab at midnight? Will I be able to spend the 30,000 zlotys given to me by another friend who traveled to Poland in 1995? (Neither he nor I knew whether it would buy me a cup of coffee or a nice dinner!)

To put the zloty question to rest, I turn to the section on money in my travel guide. The currency changed in 1997 with the old currency recognized until January 1, 1998. It's June, 1998—my friend's currency is worthless.

This brings another worry. What if the cab driver doesn't accept U.S. dollars? Even though U.S. dollars have been accepted in virtually every other country I've visited, I was obsessing about Poland. Perhaps I'm unnerved because I'm arriving alone, at midnight in a city I don't know, where the language is as foreign to me as Chinese. I try to read other sections in my travel guide, but an increasing feeling of foreboding precludes any concentration.

WHAT'S HAPPENING? THE TRAIN IS SLOWING DOWN. It seems to be stopping. It is stopping.

It's only seven o'clock. I look out the window for clues. Are we at the Polish border? Is this a passport check? All I see are trees, a grassy area, and two old buses. No buildings, no station, nothing.

After what seems an eternity, a female conductor with a friendly face enters the car and begins talking to me in a language I don't understand. She wants to see my ticket. After I hand it to her, she returns the ticket and points to the door.

I give the conductor a questioning look, most likely mixed with a little fear. She gives me a reassuring smile, points to the door and says, "Zhiv' E etz." Perhaps I'm supposed to leave the train and get on one of the buses, but why? I look up at her, point to the bus and, in a questioning voice, mimic her word, "Zhiv' E etz?" She nods and repeats, "Zhiv' E etz." To make sure I have the pronunciation right, I ask again, "Zhiv' E etz?" She patiently repeats, "Zhiv' E etz."

With no other option, I gather my luggage, tripod, and day pack and step off the train, ticket in hand. Noticeably quiet, the place seems deserted, except for a man in a plaid shirt and jeans, sprawled on a frayed lawn chair near one of the buses. I walk up to him and, with a questioning look, point to the bus, carefully mimicking the word of the train conductor, "Zhiv' E etz?" He nods. I get on the bus with my heart in my throat. No one else boards the bus.

ABOUT FIVE MINUTES LATER, THE MAN IN THE LAWN CHAIR gets behind the wheel. He maneuvers the bus onto a narrow paved road where for twenty minutes we weave through lush hills and forest, around bends and sharp curves, with houses few and far between. As we approach a town, I see a small sign. Remembering the brief Polish language lessons I took before the trip, I recognize the name on the sign, Zywiec, as "Zhiv' E etz." I feel the tension leave my body. Zywiec is a town. I bet I am to reboard the train here.

Indeed, the bus approaches the train station and stops. I gather my gear again, step off the bus, and, in high alert, begin looking for anyone who looks like a train official. I walk through the deserted station and onto the platform where I spot a man in uniform. Showing him my ticket, I point to the train and he nods. I'm a mixed bag of emotions—relief, elation, confusion.

THE RIDE INTO KRAKOW IS UNEVENTFUL. I arrive at the scheduled time and head toward the taxi stand. I cannot believe it...there is a cab!

As I walk toward the cab, I see a well-dressed woman walking toward it as well. I arrive first and begin talking with the driver who speaks a little English. He's sorry, but he cannot give me a ride; the other woman ordered the taxi. He offers to call a cab for me, which will take about a half hour to arrive.

Exhausted from the emotional upheaval of the last several hours, I thank the cab driver, looking, I'm sure, like a forlorn puppy. The well-dressed woman walks over to me and, in broken English, offers me her cab. I decline her generous gesture, saying the taxi is for her. She insists and I finally accept. I could have hugged her for her kindness.

ONCE IN THE CAB, I GIVE THE DRIVER MY HOTEL ADDRESS, which I knew was about twenty minutes away. While speeding down the abandoned thoroughfare in the dark of night, I begin to notice little neon signs in corner windows, like the signs in windows of corner bars all over the U.S. It seems as if every block has a window with the sign, "Zywiec."

After so much tension, I'm weak and giddy and begin to laugh. "Zywiec" is a beer. I'll bet the town of Zywiec has a brewery. Had I known that when I got off the bus, I might have decided to stay in Zywiec!

# My Father's Bar-B-Que
## by Karen Ackerman

The barbecue rears up out of the clearing like the Great Wall with a grill. I imagine walking up to it and running my hand along the edge of the concrete. The corner is cracked. I can see my father at a distance. I sit back in my chair. I need the distance. I don't want to think of my father this way. I don't want to know him. But it seems I have no choice. The distance is collapsing. Suddenly I'm seeing.

Everything about my father's life was small and narrow—his job, his home, his opinions. But perhaps, after what he had seen and done, that was all he wanted, all he could manage. Like many boys who graduated from high school in June 1942, he was given one option. By December, that boy who would be my father was onboard a destroyer heading out to sea. In 1952, after fighting two wars, he came ashore for good. But the boy had died. There, instead, stood a man with a wife and two kids, in need of work and a place to live.

My father took a job on an assembly line, the only peaceful thing a gunner's mate knew how to do, perhaps. And in a couple of years, we moved out of the rented double bungalow and into a place of our own. Isolated on a single acre, surrounded by corn and soybeans, woods and pasture, the house was nothing more than a hyphen, rooms in a row under a flat, tarpaper roof, a stucco shoebox with a picture window.

I remember lying in bed listening through thin walls to my father in the kitchen every morning at six. The radio tuned to WCCO, our "Good Neighbor to the Northwest," the rattle of the percolator, soon the slam of the door, the rev-rev of the Chevy, and the crunch of gravel as my father drove away. He was always home by six in the evening. He had a little setter named Patty that he loved. He would settle into a chair, my mom across the table, Patty at his feet. As far as I can remember, nothing ever changed until the summer of the barbecue, 1959.

"What was he thinking?" my husband asks. He's been listening to me talk through this piece. "Why did he build it so big?"

Every weekend that June, my father and brother drove the gravel roads between Osseo and Anoka, dragging boulders from fields and ditches with their gloved hands and heaving them into the back of the pickup. My brother was fourteen at the time. I can hear my father yelling at him. They carried the stones, one at a time, from the driveway to the far backyard. With cement and sweat, they poured a foundation, four inches thick. Someone, maybe one of our farmer-neighbors, had donated an old stove. They lifted it onto the slab. This became the iron heart around which my father and brother constructed walls, rock by rock, row upon row. On top of this they hoisted another cement slab with holes for grill and flue. Now it stood nearly chest high on my father, up to my brother's neck, and they weren't done. By the time my brother fitted the last stone to the chimney, the barbecue was four feet deep, six feet high, nine feet long. I was eight years old and could sit easily upright inside the wood box.

My father has, for the most part, disappeared. He died just before his sixty-fifth birthday, over fifteen years ago. According to his wishes, he was cremated. We dug a hole over his mother's grave and buried him there without a service. Again, that's how he wanted it. He has no headstone. My children have almost no memory of their grandfather. Until tonight, I've tried not to think about him. As for his family, it too disappeared. I haven't seen my brother in nearly ten years, even though he lives twenty minutes from me. I see my mother two or three times a year. She lives three hours north.

I do, however, go home. I feel a longing at least once a year, usually in the fall. The edges of the road have crept toward the center. I have to park a mile away and walk. The farms have disappeared, bought by the Hennepin County Park system the year I graduated from high school. Naturally, our house is gone, the foundation filled. I have difficulty locating the perimeter, the trees have grown so thick. The large rotting log must be the old elm where my swing set stood. I think those basswood are on my bed. The creek has broken its banks and spread across the lower lawn. The water is slow and murky. Nothing is as it was.

Except there, just on the outer edge of the clearing—my father's barbecue still stands like the Great Wall with a grill, except the grill has rusted through. The iron box below is filled with mud but still intact. I could build a fire.

Suddenly, I don't need to keep my distance. Suddenly I am seeing. Here is my father's headstone. Here is his monument.

# Beers of My Life: Amstel to Zywiec
## by Marla Kapperud

The great beers of my life all have a story. To understand the significance of this statement, you must understand that before the summer of 1992, I could take or leave beer. If I drank a beer, it was occasional, when social circumstances warranted. I would usually select a beer with the fewest calories and sip it with little enjoyment.

I began to enjoy beer for its flavor during a six-week trip to Central and Eastern Europe in 1992. I was thirty-nine, and this was the travel adventure I didn't have following college.

This essay begins with my trip in 1992, continues with a 1998 sojourn to Poland, and concludes with a memorable bike trip to the Czech Republic in 2000.

Each segment could be an essay in itself. If I live a long life, it's highly likely the beers of my life will become a book.

AMSTEL LIGHT, KLM BUSINESS CLASS EN ROUTE TO AMSTERDAM. My traveling companion was my good friend, Nancy. We survived grad school together and, thanks to her accumulated miles, we both were able to fly business class to our ultimate destination, Budapest.

Our flight attendant was cute, personable, and male, a nice combination.

After delivering an Amstel Light, he began chatting with us. When he learned about the last leg of my journey, a three-week trip to Russia to teach business principles to managers in Russian companies, he was intrigued.

"What are you going to teach?" he asked. I replied, "Principles of business in a market economy." Ever more curious, he asked, "What approach to economics will you use?"

As we neared Amsterdam, he asked one more question, "Do you (Americans) really need to go so far from home to teach others—can't you spend time in your own country, perhaps starting with your Vice President?"

He was referring to the then widely publicized story of Dan Quayle's very public misspelling of the word "potato" with an "e"! He smiled and we laughed.

SALZBURG. Nancy and I have very different travel requirements when it comes to lodging. Give me a clean bed, clean toilet, and a shower down the hall, and I'm happy. Nancy is used to first class all the way.

After arriving from Vienna by train, we took a cab to the Gasthof GrunerWald where I had reserved a room. After a quick glance, Nancy announced, "I can't stay here." (It had to be a quick glance, since the room was small with two double beds that essentially filled the room. The water closet was aptly named, as it was no larger than a closet. There were two bare ceiling bulbs: one in the room with the beds, the other in the WC.)

"I'm really sorry," she continued. "Would you mind if we find another hotel?" I said I didn't care. (Although I did care in one way because I was in extreme pain, having ruptured a disc in my lower back the day before in Vienna. While I didn't know my disc was ruptured, I knew I was in a lot of pain.)

Thus we went in search of a hotel about one o'clock in the afternoon. Toting our luggage behind us, carrying day packs and cameras, we stopped at all hotels that looked promising to Nancy. I waited outside while she inquired about price and cased the rooms.

Six and a half hours later, I was near the end of my stamina when we stumbled upon Hotel Ausperg. It was beautiful: marble foyer, exquisite art, tasteful décor. A young male desk clerk was attending the register. Nancy asked the room rate. "1400 schillings," he replied ($140 U.S.).

A tough negotiator, Nancy began her quest for the deal. "I heard we could get a room for 1000 schillings," she said.

"No," he replied with a winsome smile, "It's 1400 schillings."

She threw the next volley, to which he replied, "We're closed for the evening."

"Really!" Nancy replied. (Depending on the situation, Nancy

communicates a lot when she uses the word *really*. In this case, a good natured jest spiked with a bit of incredulity.) I don't remember much about the third round exchange except that he relented, agreeing to 1000 schillings. I was so grateful I could have kissed his feet.

Exhausted and grimy from hours of walking in the hot summer sun, we settled into our room, showered, and went in search of food. Even though it was only 9:30, the only restaurant serving food at that hour was around the corner. The menu was limited, but the beer was cold and oh so good. The beer was German or Austrian; the brand didn't matter. It was cold, it was good, and it celebrated the end of a very long day.

PILSNER URQUELL, PRAGUE. Nancy and I parted ways in Munich. She flew back to the States, and I boarded a train for Prague.

For six days I stayed with a high school acquaintance and his family: a wife and three children—ages six, four, and six months—in a two-bedroom flat, second level, no air conditioning.

I explored Prague during the day, coming back to a home-cooked Czech meal, boisterous children, and a stifling bedroom that smelled of sour milk. (The summer of 1992 was extraordinarily hot in Central and Eastern Europe. Humidity was high, as well—conditions that cause me to wilt at home in Minnesota.)

About two in the afternoon on day four of my stay, I was desperate for rest, shade, and something cold to drink. It was the hottest day of my journey to date, and I hadn't had an ice cold drink, let alone a beer, since my arrival.

As I walked along the Vltava, I discovered what appeared to be an elegant restaurant on an island, its tiered patio dotted with tables and umbrellas beckoning me to come, rest, enjoy the shade. A foot bridge connected me to this haven and, after finding a table, I asked the waiter for a cold beer. He brought Pilsner Urquell, a Czech beer. It was ice cold, it had body, and it was great.

To this day, I consider this the best beer of my life, not only because of its taste but because of the circumstances of that week.

BUDWEISER, ST. PETERSBURG. We had been in Russia for two hot, sultry weeks with no air conditioning and precious few cold beverages. We boarded the overnight train to St. Petersburg, arriving Saturday morning around seven o'clock. The day was a mix of morning nap, lunch, afternoon bus tour, and evening events.

After attending an extraordinary musical revue, a fellow volunteer and I returned to the hotel ready for some serious sleep. Walking down the hall toward our rooms, we heard boisterous laughter.

The revelers heard us coming. I heard my name chanted, "M-A-R-L-A." "M-A-R-L-A." As I walked into the room, my peripheral vision picked up a flying object heading toward me. It was an 18-ounce can of ice cold Budweiser, and I made the catch of my life. It did not take long to guzzle a beer I would not touch in America.

OKICIM AND ZYWIEC, POLAND, 1998. In June, 1998, I traveled to Poland for eight days. (If you read the Zywiec essay earlier in this book, an account of my anxiety-laden train trip from Bratislava to Krakow, you have the background for my desire to try this beer.) After arriving in Krakow and deducing that Zywiec was a beer, I knew I had to try it.

The evening of my first day in Krakow, I went to the bar in my hotel, the only eating establishment within walking distance. The bar was small and served a very limited menu. Voraciously hungry, I ordered a basket of chicken and Zywiec.

This beer was a slice of heaven, all half liter of it. The food order was slow in coming, so I ordered another beer. The next morning I learned that one is enough.

The next evening, I went back to the bar for my meal of the day. This time I tried another Czech beer, Okicim, a half liter. It was equally great so I ordered another, albeit smaller than a half liter.

While drinking the second beer, a man sat down at my table. He asked me a question to which I shrugged, indicating I didn't understand. He said something else, and I think I said I don't speak Polish.

I was writing in my journal at the time, "He left, thank God. Oh my God, he's back with a beer. Gulp! And now he has a friend joining him. I'll finish my beer and get the hell out of here!" Of course there's more to this story, as there always is, but Okicim is another great beer.

BUDWEISER BUDVAR, CZECH REPUBLIC, 2000. On a fourteen-day bicycle trip organized by a friend of mine, we stayed in a summer house and explored the beautiful countryside in day trips.

The owner of the summer house was named Jiri (pronounced "yizhi"). Jiri was an insurance agent, a self-styled travel agent, and the founder and guitar player in a country western band. Besides his role as host, he was paid to drive the sag wagon.

While we rarely saw him during the day, we knew he would be home to greet us when we returned from our day's explorations. Undependable in many aspects, Jiri was dependable on one account: he always kept a keg of Budweiser tapped, and he insisted we each have a glass filled all the time. We think it was an excuse to keep his glass filled...all the time. After dinner, Jiri grabbed his guitar, donned his Stetson, and entertained us with songs by Johnny Cash, Waylon Jennings, and Charley Pride.

The Budweiser I drank in St. Petersburg years earlier was not the Budweiser served at Jiri's. St. Petersburg's was definitely brewed by Anheuser Busch, a company started in the U.S. in 1852.

The original Budweiser has been brewed in Moravia, now in the Czech Republic, since the thirteenth century. Called Budweiser Budvar, the brewery is located in the town of Ceske Budejovice. We toured the brewery and imbibed this great beer in the brewery's restaurant. Jiri's keg was Budvar.

Even though the beer at Jiri's was often flat, it became the water cooler for our trip, a place to share our stories of the day.

AM I A BEER DRINKER like the stereotypical pot bellied, armchair sports fan in America? No. My motto is to let no beer touch my lips that isn't great. The beers I enjoy all have stories associated with them. When I drink them in the States, I'm reliving memories which, in the end, are one of life's greatest gifts.

# Putti
## by Gina Briefs-Elgin

After my mother's memorial Mass, a young friend confided that my mother had taught her an important life lesson—never serve cantaloupe on an orange-colored plate. I could just hear my mother: "Oh! Not *that* color, dear," my mother would have told her, deftly switching the cantaloupe slices onto Mexican blue glass. "My first thought," said my friend, "was who cares what color the plate is? But later I saw. Your mother taught me that beauty counts. She taught me that it matters how things look."

It mattered to my mother how things looked one drizzly morning on the island of Capri after early Mass. My eighty-six-year-old father had died suddenly in Italy, and my mother, as a distraction from grief, had taken two of my cousins and me on a trip she had originally planned to take with him. My grief was still dormant. The four of us, three giddy girls and my widowed mother, boarded the ferry from the sleazy, criminal docks of Naples and got off on the magical island of Capri, where my mother would commit her own crime.

Capri is famous for being one of the most beautiful islands in the world. Travel guidebooks tell me I should remember steep stone streets, whitewashed walls cascading with roses, crimson bougainvillea, yellow broom, and from every viewpoint, the luminous blue sea lying steeply below. An enchanted island! Instead I remember only three brief un-enchanted scenes, each I fervently resented then, each my cousins and I love to remember now, thirty years later.

IT WAS EARLY MORNING. I was trying to keep sleeping, but my mother was violently shaking my foot. She had turned on all the lights in our low-ceilinged hotel room and was dripping water off her raincoat onto my bedclothes.

"Gina! You've got to get up and help me right now. I've done something terrible."

I sat up fast. This pale woman frantically flinging raindrops, her grey hair wild, was so unlike my cheerful and practical British mother, whom lightning, poisonous snakes, and even war had never been able to rattle, that I was alarmed.

"I've done something awful," my mother said, sitting down hard on my feet. "I've stolen something." My heart flopped into my throat. Had my father's death unhinged her? She seemed frantic with distress and my mind filled with preposterous thoughts. Had she stolen jewelry? A gun? Had she *shot* somebody?

I scootched to the foot of the bed. Julie and Tessa and I watched as with shaking hands she opened her straw bag and removed an object hidden under her scarf. "Oh, dear," she said, unveiling the object of her crime. And here it was—a five-inch-high pink plastic dashboard mascot of a roguish little boy. He was holding his outsized dick in his hand and pissing into a little toilet. By means of the handle on the toilet, the penis of this fiendish boy could be ratcheted up or down. Coming out of early morning Mass, glowing with the beauty of the sacrament and the fresh Capri dawn, my mother had stepped into a shop to buy postcards. This hideous toy, grinning at her from the cash register, had struck her like a blow. She had told the shopkeeper it was a shame to have such a thing in such a beautiful setting. She had offered to buy it from him. "No, no," he had said, shrugging, "it was a present from a friend." And then he had turned his back. It had taken her only a moment to commit her crime, to swish the ugly thing into her big straw bag and hurry out into the wet street.

I was outraged and pushed her off my feet. For this she got me up? But my mother was in a frenzy of anxiety.

"What if he saw me!" she said. "What if he told the police? What if it gets into the papers?" She imagined the headlines for us, something like this: "Professor's Widow Steals Obscene Toy."

"Gina," she said, "you've got to go right now and explain to that man. Apologize for me."

Now I was scared. Was my mother coming unglued? Why did she have to go and do this crazy thing? And now she wanted me to fix it. But I was proving good at denial these days. "I need more sleep," I told her. "I'll take it back later."

"We're not *taking* it back," she said. "I just want you to explain to the man and apologize for me. Tell him his island of Capri is so beautiful that he shouldn't have such an ugly thing on his cash register. It doesn't belong. Offer to pay for it." She opened her wallet, her British self again, mustering her troop.

"It doesn't *matter* what's on a store's cash register," I argued, exasperated now. "It's his store."

"Yes, it does," said my mother firmly, "it's ugly and we're not giving it back." She wasn't suffering from madness after all, I realized, just grief and offended aesthetics.

Resentfully, I got out of my cozy bedclothes. With very bad grace, I took the envelope of *lire* my mother handed me. Perhaps I even looked up *crazy* in the Italian dictionary. Then I put on my shorts and sweater and stepped out onto the drizzly street. I was aware that I was being a graceless daughter, that Julie or Tessa, who were devoted to my mother, would have embraced the mission of clearing her name. But I was the one who spoke a little Italian. I walked across the cobbles towards the shop, rehearsing my speech, full of dread. And then an idea occurred to me—a way to postpone the moment of walking into the shop. A gesture that might almost redeem me in my own eyes. Minutes ticked by as I ducked in and out of tourist shops, hoping that my cousins were worrying at my delay and not enjoying breakfast without me. At last I lit on another boy-statue, this one a terracotta cherub, genderless, mostly wings.

Armed with my bland cherub, I crossed the street and walked fast into the pillaged shop and straight to the counter before I could lose my courage. But the shopkeeper was talking to a friend, which gave me time to be nervous, time to look at the cash register, where the nasty boy must have been, time to wonder—absurdly—how the shopkeeper could even keep shop, as though nothing had happened, with his interesting mascot missing from right under his eye. Time to wonder whether he knew already the reason that brought me here, while he chatted deliberately on and on.

Finally, the friend moved away from the cash register. I stepped forward, my cherub in hand. I pushed the envelope of *lire* across the counter, and then I unwrapped the cherub. "This is for you, signor," I told him. "My mother," I said, pointing to the empty spot, "has stolen your boy. She is *matta*, crazy," I told him in broken Italian, dancing my fingers on either side of my face to show him crazy. "My father is dead," I told him.

"*Bene, bene*, it's all right," he told me, mostly bored. But I pressed the modest cherub on him.

"*Non, signorina.*" He didn't want it and tried to give it back to me.

"Take it!" I said, and fled from the shop. In the drizzly street I cried for a long time, for my father, for my mother, for my unkindness in not recognizing her theft as a symptom of grief. Then I wiped my eyes and went back to the *pensione*.

On the night we left Capri, my cousins and I leaned over the white ferry railing. The black water was foaming far below us as we ploughed away from the magical island, and we had a job to do. "Here he is!" said Julie. In a moment, she and Tessa were merrily balancing the toy on the railing, pushing the tiny tank handle up and down a last few times. My mother's crime and my own unsympathetic heart embarrassed me still, but then I was laughing too, as the three of us, with a giddy hoot, consigned the unzipped boy to the waves.

# Reclamation
## by Pamela Mittlefehldt

The family all said it was a combination of lousy diet and loneliness that drove Uncle Carl mad—raw soybeans and absolute isolation for almost two years. Nutritional and social starvation. But I suspected it was the ghosts.

THE REST OF THE FAMILY had abandoned the farm years before—marrying, dying, moving to New York City. Carl, the one who had always resented it the most, was left by default. It could have been the land that smothered his dreams—the cyclic monotony of spreading manure, planting, pulling corn from soybeans, pulling soybeans from corn, praying through drought, getting the harvest in before the rain came. Never making enough to get ahead. But I think it was the rage of spirits that strangled his dreams. "This is how it feels," they keened. "This is what we lost."

Ottawa, Illinois. The town retains the name of the first people. The land retains their souls. When my father was a boy, spring plowing turned up hundreds of arrowheads. But that wasn't all that lingered. The land was drenched in sorrow.

My grandparents settled this place, "just off the boat," as they said—German immigrants for whom English remained a foreign language,

America a foreign land. They managed to buy these 160 acres across from the Illinois River, just down the road from Starved Rock.

The legend of Starved Rock flickered through my childhood nightmares. A battle between the Ottawa and the Pottawattamie Indians. The Ottawa warriors were trapped on the high limestone cliff, while their enemies surrounded them on the ground below, waiting and watching while they slowly starved or plunged to their death on the rocks. They all died.

It was a hardscrabble farm in the midst of rich farming country, a place that leeched the life from everything on it. Cows died without calving. Milk soured before it came through the separator. The well went dry every summer. Chickens refused to lay. The corn turned parchment before the tassels dried.

But I loved that farm. I spent my summers there, learning how to reach under hens in search of eggs, riding on the back of the tractor behind my uncle as he plowed the upper forty. I tromped through the timber in search of the foxes my uncle promised were there. Only one place refused to take me in. The waterfall.

A small creek meandered through the land. Just behind the farmhouse, it plunged over the limestone in a thready waterfall. It didn't drop more than thirty feet, but the glen it had created over the centuries was a world apart. There was no path down, which always struck me as strange. This was the most beautiful place on the farm, and yet it seemed that no one but me ever went there. I would skid down the steep hill, trying to slow my descent by clutching tall weeds and roots. At the bottom, the world was shadowed, green, and dank. The ground was boggy. Rocks were slick with furry moss. The falls splattered into a small pool that absorbed all the water and sucked it mysteriously into the ground. Behind the waterfall, a hollowed out cave gaped like a skull's mouth. It was a restless place—muted, eerily silent except for the splat and trickle of water. And the voices. Sometimes a low moan rolled from the cave. Sometimes a sigh so drenched in sadness it wrenched my heart. Sometimes the echoing shadow of murmuring voices. I never recognized words. They spoke a lexicon of loss and grief. And always, they drove me up the cliff in a mad-dash scramble of terror and longing. I would burst into the lazy heat of summer, my skin chilled and slick from the breath of ghosts.

After Carl's funeral, Will and I decided to spend a night at the farm, rather than drive the three hours back to Chicago. The house was still there, but the fields had stood fallow for years. The chicken coop had half collapsed. The barn doors had fallen off, and the roof was riddled with holes. We decided to set up a tent in the drive, right beside the house. It was dusk, and slowly my skin began feeling clammy, even though the air was still August steamy. I could faintly hear the splatter of tumbling water. A sudden wind blew through the barnyard, rustling the dried weeds around the pump, rattling the metal siding on the corncrib. Branches moaned against each other. A pressure began building in my head. "Get out." My pulse beat against my temples. "Leave. Now."

I sat at the opening of the tent, wondering if I would feel safer zipped inside. Finally, feeling like an idiot, I turned to Will. "How would it be if we headed back to the city tonight?" I expected a bit of ridiculing resistance. He glanced at me, and simply said, "I thought you'd never suggest it." We were gone in less than ten minutes.

I didn't return to the farm for years. By then, the outbuildings had disintegrated into jagged piles of fractured lumber. Vagrants had broken into the house, lighting fires that eventually had burned a hole from the root cellar right up through the living room ceiling. I walked outside, taking photographs. A rusted tractor, with goldenrod growing up through the spokes. The pump, with a dribble of moss oozing from the spout. Clouds framed by gaping holes— all that remained of the barn roof. I finally went inside, stepping cautiously around the scorched holes in the floor. The kitchen had been gutted of everything except the old iron pump and the hulking cookstove. A rusted blue and white ladle lay on the floor next to the enamel bucket that had held the drinking water.

The last picture I took was of a row of hooks by the back door. Each hook held a piece of Uncle Carl's clothing. Stained overalls, a woolen jacket, a ripped blue shirt that still smelled of grease and sweat, pollen and sunlight. When the photos came back, I was chilled as I studied that final shot. From each piece of clothing, a gauzy streak of light rose and stretched towards the ceiling. The land had finally had its way. The very last of us was gone.

# Death Toll Mounts In Vietnam
## by Catherine Watson
### Special to the Star Tribune

"Accident victims' families are worse—they're not prepared. Military families are calmer. They're half expecting it."

THE SPEAKER WAS A VETERAN JOURNALIST, giving advice to me and a handful of other young reporters nearly 40 years ago, as we worked on a gruesome task, in another ugly war. Every time I read a headline about American deaths in Iraq, I remember those words. I've been remembering them a lot lately.

We were night-siders on the old Minneapolis Tribune, working shifts that started in late afternoon and went on till 10 or 12 at night. All of us were women. On the surface, that seemed a triumph of feminism—lots of women entering what had traditionally been a male profession.

The real reason had to do with the Vietnam War. Women weren't draftable, so hiring us meant that the newspaper—and plenty of other American businesses—didn't have to keep a job open for a guy who'd gotten drafted off the staff.

Because we were cub reporters, we did the grunt work, which included making phone calls to sheriff's offices about tornado damage, snow conditions, the size of hailstones in distant counties and, inevitably, fatal traffic accidents, drownings and murders.

Somewhere in late 1966, as the numbers of dead and missing began to steepen in Vietnam, our city editor, Stu Baird, called us together and announced a new assignment.

From that point on until the war was over, Baird said, the Tribune would publish a small profile of each soldier lost from our region. "These are young men dead before their time," he said. "We are not going to let them go in silence."

It was our job to gather the information. Every day, the Department of Defense prepared a list of those killed in action or identified as missing in action, and the Associated Press sent that list to daily papers across the country.

Along with hundreds of other stories, the list was churned out of a teletype machine. You can still hear their clanking in the background of old movies about this business—it used to be the dominant sound of the newsroom.

Copy aides ripped the incoming stories off the teletypes and carried them to the editors, who decided which ones would get into the next morning's paper. The daily list from the Department of Defense was passed on to one of us. We referred to what we did next as "calling the Vietnam dead."

The AP list gave only the basics: name, rank and home town. If the name was unusual and the town small, you could often get the right family just by phoning Information. In other cases, or when there were a lot of, say, Andersons or Swensons to choose from, we called the sheriff's office, the police, or even the local weekly and asked which family this man belonged to. Somebody always knew. Then we called the family.

We quickly developed a standard introduction: apologize for disturbing them at this time, say we are sorry for their loss, explain that the paper wanted to honor their soldier, ask if they would help us with information. They always said, "Yes."

"Military families are calmer..." I don't remember which old reporter told me that, but it was true. Only "calm" wasn't quite the right word. "Numb" was more like it. Numb and resigned.

I remember talking to 18-year-old widows, to young mothers about to have their first child, to parents, to siblings, sometimes a fiancée, grandparents, aunts, uncles. They seldom became emotional on the phone.

The profiles were short, just a paragraph or two—there were so many that the paper didn't have room for anything longer—and that meant the interviews were mercifully brief. Where was your husband/son/father/brother when you last heard from him? How long had your husband/son/father/brother been in Vietnam? Do you have a recent photo of your husband/son/father/brother?

The names of the dead and missing weren't supposed to be released to the press until the DOD had notified the next of kin. But the military is very big, and sometimes it makes mistakes.

One night, when one of the other women was doing the calling, she reached a family that hadn't been notified yet. Her phone call broke the news. It was what we all dreaded, and I remember being grateful that it hadn't been me.

My turn came soon enough, in a different way, and it was my fault, not the DOD's. It still makes my skin crawl and my stomach tighten.

The AP list was difficult to read-single-spaced, typed in fuzzy capitals on rough paper. It had two parts, barely separated: KILLED IN ACTION and MISSING IN ACTION. I had not known how much hope lay hidden in the second heading, until a night when I misread the list and got the wrong line.

"This is the Minneapolis Tribune," I said to one of those strangely calm young widows. "The Associated Press has informed us that your husband is missing in action and ..."

The girl gasped. "Missing!" she said. "MISSING! They told me he was dead!"

I knew instantly what had happened and felt shivery and sick. "No, no!" I said. "They told you the truth! I read it wrong! I'm sorry! I'm so sorry!"

She did not break down or get angry. She took a deep breath, the numb tone came back into her voice, and she answered all the usual questions.

I do not remember crying about it then, but it has made me cry many times since, including now. Maybe especially now, when the same phone calls are being made to another generation of grieving families, the same advice being given to young reporters about how to handle them and the same stories written about what they say.

Each time I read one, I remember that young widow, and I am sorry all over again—more than a thousand times sorry, so far, and counting.

This essay was first published in the Minneapolis Star Tribune.

## Acknowledgements

No book gets published without a lot of hard work. This book is no exception. At the end of our Travel Writing class in July 2004, Marla Kapperud organized a group that made it happen. The editorial board consisted of Maureen Breitzmann, Virginia Broich, Jean Comstock, Marla Kapperud and Laura Langer. Each served as an editor, and Laura created the design. Their work made this book what it is today. Early on, we made the decision to leave each writer's work intact, preserving her unique vision of place and spirit and memory. The editors provided a final look at the presentation of each work.

We wish to thank our classmates and fellow contributors for their inspiring essays, and for their patience and support. The University of Minnesota's Split Rock Arts Program deserves the credit for bringing us together in Catherine Watson's class, providing the creative climate—as twenty years of Program participants can attest.

Finally, we want to thank Catherine Watson for her contribution and her sincere belief that we all are writers with stories to tell.

# Contributors

KAREN ACKERMAN saw three of her four children graduate in 2005—two from college and one from high school, leaving her free to "consider her options." She began writing fiction for middle-grade readers ten years ago, in addition to her travel and memoir writing. She and her husband Joel live in Eden Prairie in a nearly empty nest.

MAUREEN BREITZMANN is originally from Superior, Wisconsin, but is currently settled in Minneapolis, Minnesota. She earned a bachelor's degree in English Literature at the University of Wisconsin-Eau Claire, and her work periodically appears in the Minneapolis Star Tribune. She would love to quit her 9 to 5 and see the world before settling down to write a book.

GINA BRIEFS-ELGIN lives in Northern New Mexico with her husband and son, both artists. She teaches composition and creative writing at New Mexico Highlands University. Her favorite reading is creative nonfiction, especially travel writing; Dickens; The Thousand and One Nights; eastern mysticism; and Life on the Mississippi. Other than home with her family, her favorite place in the world to be is on a train.

VIRGINIA BROICH found retirement from the rat race of a school system in June 2004 freeing. Since then, she has pursued a writing life. In 2005, she published ten articles in The Old Times antique newspaper. She lives with her encouraging husband and their 13-year-old cockatiel Pretty in Northeast Minneapolis.

JEAN COMSTOCK was one of those obnoxious children who actually enjoyed writing assignments in school. Now, after working with computers and puzzling over software all day, she still enjoys her writing time. She shares an old Victorian home with permanent, full-time cats Burton and Beijing, and several guest (foster) cats in historic Dayton's Bluff above downtown Saint Paul, Minnesota.

JANE CONGDON grew up in West Virginia. She now lives and works in the Cincinnati area. Jane is a veteran of writing workshops at Ghost Ranch in New Mexico as well as Split Rock. She won the 2005 Story Contest sponsored by Macabi Skirt. Jane's writing focus is nonfiction, including travel. At the time of this publication, she was planning a trip to Romania.

MAGGIE DELFOSSE lives with her husband in Wisconsin, where she works as a freelance editor of non-fiction books and aspires to write both fiction and nonfiction stories of journeying.

MARLA KAPPERUD first learned about distance during her childhood on a dry land wheat farm in Montana, where neighbors were few and far between and the horizon always far away. She discovered books at an early age and learned that a world outside the golden waves of grain existed. After a move to Minneapolis to finish her baccalaureate degree, she discovered the joy of travel one summer and hasn't stopped since.

LAURA LANGER divides her time between work as a marketing director, volunteering, dreams of travel, and friends and family. She enjoys travel for its own sake, and finds the practice of travel writing like "seeing and touching it all again." She lives in Minneapolis, where she is endlessly finishing her first novel.

MARY McCONNON was born and raised in Winona, Minnesota. Retired twice, once from teaching high school social studies, and a second time from being an office manager, she is now a volunteer teacher of conversational English to foreign students and visiting scholars at UC Berkeley. She travels as "often as I can afford." A recent trip was experienced from a small barge traveling through the rivers and canals of Provence.

PAMELA MITTLEFEHLDT retired after years of teaching American Studies and Community Studies at St. Cloud State University to focus on her writing. She is fascinated with writing about the mystery and meaning of place in our lives. She finally lives in a place she loves-Duluth, Minnesota.

MARY LOUISE POQUETTE is a geographer and freelance writer. An "airline brat," she caught the travel bug early. Her less high-tech methods of getting from place to place include horses, canoes and sailboats.

SUSAN SLATER BLYTHE gave up teaching American Literature at a technical college, and is now writing a memoir. She is pictured on her fifth birthday when she received a two wheel bike and her first diary. Residing in the Midwest, she still rides a bike, journals daily and seeks others who notice the important stuff.

DIANE SMITH lives in Minneapolis. During the day, she makes her living as a nurse, but when night arrives, you can find her dreaming of life on the lakes and portages of the BWCA.

CATHERINE WATSON is the former travel editor of the Minneapolis Star Tribune. She divides her home time between Minneapolis and Galena, Illinois, and is at work on an historical travel memoir. Catherine published her first book, *Roads Less Traveled: Dispatches from the Ends of the Earth*, a collection of her award-winning travel essays, in 2005.

KELLY WESTHOFF is a writer from the Twin Cities. She covers local women's issues for the Minnesota Women's Press. In addition, she writes for other area publications. She loves to travel and would venture just about anywhere. Stamps in her passport include Argentina, Bolivia, Guatemala, Cuba, Italy, Spain and more. Currently she is on a seven-month round the world tour with her husband.

BRENDA WOLFE is dancing, laughing, and living in St. Paul.